D1112330

# W. E. B. DuBOIS

# W.E.B. DuBOIS

## PATRICIA AND FREDRICK McKISSACK

*Franklin Watts*
*New York/London/Toronto/Sydney*
*An Impact Biography/1990*

"If We Must Die" by Claude McKay is reprinted with the permission of Twayne Publishers, a division of G. K. Hall & Co., Boston.

"The Negro Speaks of Rivers" copyright by Alfred A. Knopf, Inc. and renewed 1954 by Langston Hughes. Reprinted from *Selected Poems of Langston Hughes* by permission of the publisher.

Photographs courtesy of: Brown Brothers: p. 2; New York Public Library: pp. 13, 14, 46, 70, 81, 82 (all Schomburg Center), 31 (Picture Collection); Wide World Photos: pp. 53, 106, 111,118,126,131; UPI/ Bettmann Newsphotos: p. 85.

Library of Congress Cataloging-in-Publication Data

McKissack, Pat, 1944–
W.E.B. DuBois / Patricia and Fredrick McKissack.
p. cm. — (An Impact biography)
Includes bibliographical references and index.
Summary: Examines the upbringing, education, writings, and political activities of one of the founders of the NAACP.
ISBN 0-531-10939-9
1. Du Bois, W. E. B. (William Edward Burghardt), 1868–1963—Juvenile literature. 2. Afro-Americans—United States—Biography—Juvenile literature. 3. Civil rights workers—United States—Biography—Juvenile literature. 4. National Association for the Advancement of Colored People—Biography—Juvenile literature. 5. Afro-Americans—Historiography—Juvenile literature. [1. Du Bois, W. E. B. (William Edward Burghardt), 1868–1963. 2. Civil rights workers. 3. Afro-Americans—Biography.] I. McKissack, Fredrick. II. Title.
E185.97.D73M45 1990
303.48′4′092—dc20
[B]     [92]     90-37823 CIP AC

To our sons,
Fred, Robert and John McKissack

# CONTENTS

# W. E. B. DuBOIS

# one

## THE EARLY YEARS

At the March on Washington, August 28, 1963, Roy Wilkins, executive director of the National Association for the Advancement of Colored People (NAACP), announced that W.E.B. DuBois (pronounced Du-Boyce), the great African-American writer, educator, historian, and civil rights leader, had died the night before in Ghana, West Africa.

At the historic March on Washington a quarter of a million Americans—belonging to all races and from different religious affiliations, economic and educational backgrounds—took a dramatic stand against racial injustice. For years W.E.B. DuBois had been in the forefront of the struggle for social and political justice all over the world. The sad irony was that *he* wasn't one of the many speakers to urge the crowd to work for a better America, where the rights guaranteed by the United States Constitution would be fairly applied, to all citizens, regardless of race. It was to this end that DuBois had dedicated his life's work. To many of the protestors, DuBois's absence was especially felt and his death announcement particularly moving because they knew the old warrior's story and why he had chosen to live and die so far away from home.

Filling in the blanks between DuBois's birth in 1868 and his death in 1963 is an unforgettable ninety-five-year saga of one man's dedication, determination, disappointment and triumph in the continuing struggle for worldwide human rights.

The story began February 23, 1868. William Edward Burghardt DuBois was born in Great Barrington, Massachusetts. Millions of slaves had been freed during the Civil War, but that event had little effect on the free people of color who had been living in the Berkshire County area since revolutionary times. Having never been slaves, nor the children of slaves, DuBois's parents were never shackled by the physical or mental chains of the plantation system. It was into this free and independent African-American family that W.E.B. DuBois was born.[1]

Mary Silvina Burghardt, DuBois's mother, could trace her ancestry to an African who, in about 1730, had been captured by Dutch slave traders and sold to the Burghardt family. The slave child was given the name Tom Burghardt.

Tom served as a private in the Revolutionary War. Afterward, he was awarded his freedom, and given land on the South Egremont plain in the Berkshires. Tom's son Othello married Sally Lampman, and they were the parents of Mary, who was born January 14, 1831.[2]

DuBois's father was also a member of the proud New England free black society. Jacques DuBois, a French Huguenot, migrated to Kingston, New York, in the early seventeenth century. He was the son of Chrétien DuBois of Wicres in French Flanders. Jacques's son, Dr. James DuBois, lived in the Bahama Islands, where he fathered two sons by his

*Childhood home of DuBois
in Great Barrington,
Massachusetts. DuBois's
family were free northerners
who did not know the
experience of slavery.*

Bahamian common-law wife. (They lived together as husband and wife but they were never legally married.) After the mother's death in about 1810, Dr. DuBois brought his sons, Alexander and John, to the United States. Because of the boys' fair skin, and Dr. DuBois's affection for them, Alexander and John were accepted as white children, and educated in a fine Connecticut boys' school. [3]

Unfortunately, Dr. DuBois died of a stroke in about 1820, leaving no will. His sons were exposed as the illegitimate offspring of a black slave woman, and therefore, not entitled to any legal claim on the DuBois estate. In fact, they were considered fortunate to have been allowed to keep their freedom. They could have been sold into slavery.

The brothers were separated, farmed out as apprentices by a greedy relative who wanted to secure the DuBois estate for himself. Whatever happened to John is unknown. Alexander, however, served as a shoemaker's apprentice until 1823, when he married Sarah Marsh Lewis and moved to Haiti.

Shortly after giving birth to two sons, Augusta and Alfred, Sarah DuBois died. Alexander returned to the United States with his sons and soon remarried.

Alfred grew up to be a "Jack-of-all-trades," traveling from place to place, making a living as a barber, a merchant, and even a preacher. After serving in the Civil War, Alfred DuBois, who was then forty-

*DuBois's mother, Mary Burghardt DuBois, instilled in her son a drive to obtain a first-rate education.*

two, came to Great Barrington, where he met and married Mary Burghardt, who was thirty-six. From this union was born W.E.B. DuBois.[4]

Mary Burghardt DuBois has been described as "brown and rather small with smooth skin and lovely eyes and hair that curled down each side of her forehead from the part in the middle." Of his father, DuBois said he was "always irresponsible but charming," unlike the boy's grandfather Alexander DuBois, who was strict and formal.

To everyone's disappointment, Alfred was a wanderer. His marriage to Mary didn't last too long. Unable to settle into the routine of married life or to accept his paternal responsibilities, Alfred deserted his family when young Will was still a toddler.[5]

Mary returned to the Burghardt farm, but she stayed only until Will reached school age. Then she moved back into Great Barrington where her son could receive a proper education. Education was important to the proud, free black people of that region. Mary DuBois adhered to what most people of the nineteenth century believed: education was the key to success. Wealth, in her opinion, was the result of commitment, hard work and personal sacrifice. The poor were either lazy or the victims of circumstance, and in most cases, bad circumstances could be reversed if the twin virtues—hard work and thrift—were practiced to the letter. Mary DuBois instilled this philosophy in her young son's mind. Years later, DuBois would say of his mother, "She was rather silent, but very determined . . ." An apt description of himself as well.[6]

To keep young Will in school, Mary took in laundry and did domestic work. And when he was older, Will helped supplement the family income by doing chores and running errands for neighbors and local businessmen. When free to play, he enjoyed the games of Great Barrington youth—ice skating on Mansfield Pond, coasting down Castle Hill, playing Indians, and exploring the brook that ran past his house.

Racial segregation wasn't practiced. The color line in the small New England town was so faint people crossed over it without doubt or fear. For example, Miss Maria Baldwin, a black woman, taught hundreds of white students as well as the handful of blacks who attended her classes. There were, however, strict social and economic codes that were followed rigidly. The rich and well-educated simply did not socialize with the poor and ignorant. Will was poor, but he was accepted among Great Barrington's best families because of his intellect, keen wit, and ambition.

In school or at play, Will was rarely treated differently because of his color or his poverty. His high school principal, Frank S. Hosmer, had recognized DuBois's potential and had expressed confidence in the boy's ability to others. For a student who was already highly motivated, this kind of special attention encouraged him to excel.

Though never much of an athlete, he was unrivaled in discourse, argumentation and debate. He was a gifted speaker whose confidence sometimes borderlined on arrogance. But, just as his mother had predicted, his grades earned him the continued respect of his peers, and recognition from community leaders and businessmen.

While still in high school, Will became a correspondent to the *New York Globe*, published by T. Thomas Fortune, a pioneer in African-American journalism.

The launching of DuBois's long journalism career began during the summer of his senior year of high school. He got a peek outside the provincial world of the Berkshires while visiting his grandfather Alexander DuBois in New Bedford, Massachusetts. He hadn't seen his grandfather since early childhood, but the old man left a lasting impression. Will described him as "a formidable figure—short, thickset, taciturn, curt but civil; awesome with the dignity of eighty years." Alexander had worked as a steward on the New York–New Haven boat line, and had also owned a grocery store. DuBois wrote about this adventure, and the story was published in the *Globe*. After that, he became a regular contributor to the paper.

In 1884, DuBois, along with eleven of his fellow classmates, graduated from Great Barrington High School with honors. At that time graduation from high school was rare for both black and white students. Years later, DuBois would describe the motivation behind his desire for an education. "I was brought up from my earliest years with the idea of regular attendance at school. The curriculum was simple—reading, writing, spelling and arithmetic, grammar, geography and history. We learned the alphabet; we were drilled rigorously on the multiplication table and we drew accurate maps. We could spell correctly and read clearly."[7]

Although he called it "simple," his college preparatory curriculum had been rigorous, requiring him to take four years of Latin and three of Greek, math, history, physiology and hygiene.

The townspeople of Great Barrington knew that Will DuBois was no ordinary high school graduate and the lack of money should not stop his continued education. With the help of a few benefactors, he was given a scholarship to Fisk University in Nashville, Tennessee.

Though grateful, his black friends were deeply concerned. Why not Harvard instead of Fisk? The South was considered the front door to hell, and the idea of a black person voluntarily going there was unthinkable. But, the scholarship was available for Fisk or nowhere. More than anything, DuBois hungered for knowledge, even if he had to go south to find it. So, he reasoned that going to Fisk would offer him a unique opportunity to learn more about the African-American experience. How bad could that be?

In the midst of his preparations to leave for college, his mother died, at age fifty-four. Whenever he spoke or wrote about her in future years, it would be with great love and deep appreciation.

A DuBois biographer, Francis L. Broderick, stated Mary DuBois was ". . . a simple and untutored woman. She had left young Will her pride in a family tree since revolutionary times, and her ambition for his success. To his credit, DuBois remembered this legacy with deep gratitude."[8]

With his mother's philosophy deeply embedded in his psyche, seventeen-year-old Will DuBois left Great Barrington behind and set out for Tennessee in the fall of 1885. It was the second time he had been away from the sheltered town of his birth. Going "down home" for William Edward Burghardt DuBois was a rude awakening—a realization of just how bad life could be for people of color.

# two

## THE FISK EXPERIENCE

After the Civil War, millions of former slaves found themselves in a hostile environment. Angry whites didn't want to accept their former slaves as equals, and only reluctantly participated in any projects designed to better the conditions of the newly freed. Blacks, who were unable to take full advantage of freedom because they lacked education, money, tools, and job opportunities, found themselves drifting back into servitude, out of need, more than desire.

Knowing help would never come from southern leadership, the Reconstruction Congress tried to alleviate the pressing problems by establishing the Freedmen's Bureau, on March 3, 1865.

Historian Lerone Bennett describes the bureau's functions as a combination of the "Urban League, WPA, CIO, and War on Poverty all wrapped up into a prototypical NAACP."[9]

Some, but not all, of the first southern black colleges were started as a result of Freedmen's Bureau money. Grant proposals were submitted by northern white churches whose administration promised to supplement the federal grant, and to provide management and staff. The idea was to train former slaves so that, in time, the school's administration could be turned over to them. The black community strongly supported these early educational institutions by holding fund-raisers, making donations and enrolling their children, no matter what financial sacrifice had to be made.

Fisk University, located in Nashville, Tennessee, was founded in 1866 by the American Missionary Society combined with aid from the Freedmen's Bureau. Other well-known black colleges were also started during this period: Atlanta College, Virginia Union, and Lincoln in Missouri to name a few of the oldest.

According to an 1884–85 school brochure, Fisk University aimed "to thoroughly establish among the colored youth the conviction of the absolute necessity of patient, long-continued, exact and comprehensive work in preparation for high positions and large responsibilities."[10]

Language of that kind was impressive to an ambitious young man like W.E.B. DuBois. Academically he was ready for the challenges of college work. He was admitted as a sophomore because of his outstanding high school record. But, the young New Englander of African and French Huguenot descent was not ready for the new environment he was exposed to in the South.

For the first time Will collided head on with white supremacy, race hatred, and discrimination. He had no problems with Fisk's white administration and faculty such as Erastus Cravath, the president, William Morris and Mrs. Lucy Green, two of his favorite professors. Adam Spence, who taught him Greek, and Thomas A. Chase, who taught him natural sciences, have been credited as being among the most influential people in his academic life. For the most part, the white staff treated the all-black student population with respect. But DuBois was shocked to discover that poor, illiterate whites thought themselves superior to him *based entirely upon skin color.*[11]

He wrote later: "I was tossed boldly into the 'Negro Problem' . . . I suddenly came to a region where the world was split into white and black halves, and where the darker half was held back by race prejudice and legal bonds, as well as by deep ignorance and dire poverty."[12]

From his first encounter to his last, DuBois never wavered in his unyielding opposition to any form of racism. And he didn't hesitate to voice his opinions about race relations openly, admonishing blacks for surrendering their personhood based on irrational prejudice, and criticizing learned whites for not taking a firmer stand against racial intolerance.

Although deeply troubled by racism, DuBois thoroughly enjoyed his exposure to an all-black academic environment. At Great Barrington High School, he had been the youngest and the only non-white member of his class. At Fisk, thirty-five students, some of them former slaves and ten years his senior, were enrolled in the college department. He marveled at the various skin complexions, eye colors, and hair textures. He was delighted to see other blacks who were intelligent, talented, and gifted, too. Never before had he seen so many beautiful people united for the purpose of "bettering the race" through education.

His classmates were also fascinated by the outspoken black yankee who looked white men straight in the eye and thought of himself as any man's equal. Some of his peers, having lived as slaves, were intimidated by white leadership and fearful about being too assertive. This attitude interested young Will.

DuBois grew intensely curious about slavery. He probed for information, and without fail, the chilling stories of inhuman treatment touched him deeply. Through his classmates he experienced vicariously what he later described as "every phrase of insult and repression" of slavery.[13]

He also learned about the spirituals. The Fisk Jubilee Singers had made the world aware of the songs composed in the cotton fields and kitchens of the antebellum South. The haunting words and unique rhythms of these songs opened a window onto a world DuBois knew nothing about. In his essay "Of the Sorrow Songs," DuBois would later write that the spirituals were "the music of an unhappy people, of the children of disappointment; they tell us of death and suffering and unvoiced longing toward a truer world of misty wanderings and hidden ways."[14]

The songs were a legacy of his people's suffering, a comfort to them during their bondage. It delighted him to know that the spirituals had been used to send messages, much the same way their African ancestors had communicated with the drum. The slaves had had their own way of knowing when a spiritual was being sung in a religious way or as a message. To other listeners, there was no discernible difference. For example, the lyrics to "Steal Away," sung a certain way, told other slaves that one among them was going to make a run for freedom that night.

Soon, these casual conversations with his peers grew into an insatiable desire to academically confront racism and crush it with scientific truth. Listening to both stories and songs helped DuBois better understand slavery. Bondage, he determined, was crippling to both the master and the slave.

Inside the walls of Fisk, young DuBois was surrounded by liberal whites, and blacks he believed were the "advance guard of the Negro civilizing army." Outside was the other South, where hatred, bigotry, fear, and poverty ruled supreme. DuBois avoided contact with whites outside the college walls. But, for two summers, he worked as a teacher in Wilson County, about 35 miles from Nashville. He was paid thirty dollars for two months' service in a "school" that was little more than a shack with a dirt floor.

He held classes in elementary writing, reading, and arithmetic. Grateful for the opportunity, poor sharecroppers sent their children to school, even though their children's hands were needed in the fields. Each day a sharecropper's child spent in school cut into the family's meager earnings. For many poor farmers, getting their children an education was worth any sacrifice. This grass root dedication to education was uplifting to the young student, but equally discouraging to him was the poverty and ignorance which remained when the summer ended.

After his fieldwork, DuBois believed he had found the key to combating racism. In summarizing his summer, he wrote, "overt racism was the misbegotten child of ignorance; therefore, education was the cure for the race problem." He felt it was the obligation of his generation to carry out the next stage of black emancipation: independent problem-solving, critical thinking and developing political savvy. To this end DuBois invested a great deal of energy.

In a short story written in 1887, DuBois set forth his theory that discrimination could not coexist with education. Well-read people would not allow racial prejudice to cloud their reason. In that same year, he wrote "An Open Letter to the Southern People," in which he pointed out that southern blacks were being denied the right to vote in spite of the Fifteenth Amendment on the grounds that they were ignorant. Black ignorance, he argued, was the result of white ignorance, terrorism and intimidation. DuBois asserted that enlightened, fair-minded southern whites and the growing educated black population should work together to overcome the problems of racism and discrimination.[15]

Those around him quickly realized that DuBois had reached a level of independent judgment and political maturity many of his peers had not yet attained. For example, he argued if blacks voted thoughtfully rather than predictably they might be given more consideration by both political parties. President Grover Cleveland, a Democrat, had been trying to woo blacks away from the Republican party, and had, in large measure, shown support for black causes. At twenty, DuBois presented a speech at an intercollegiate convention, suggesting that blind allegiance to the Republican party was little more than political slavery. Abraham Lincoln had been a Republican, and for years blacks were unquestioningly loyal to the party of the "Great Emancipator." Frederick Douglass, who was at that time the most respected African-American leader, had said it would be better to divide the black vote between "Light and darkness, truth and error, Heaven and Hell" as to divide it between Republicans and Democrats. The young Fisk student disagreed.

In addition to being a public speaker, and student leader, DuBois also became the editor of the *Fisk Herald*, and he organized a male glee club which earned money working and singing at hotels.

Although he was involved in a lot of extra-curricular activities which the staff encouraged, DuBois's scholarship remained constant. In his first year, he studied the *Iliad*, the *Odyssey* and the Bible written in Greek, along with French grammar and literature, botany, rhetoric, and calculus. The following year, he read Livy and Tacitus along with Demosthenes' *Oration on the Crown* and Sophocles' *Antigone*, German grammar and translations, physiology, hygiene and astronomy. During his last year, DuBois studied James Boscom's *Science and Mind*, and James McCosh's *Laws of Discursive Thought*. He rounded out his senior year with ethics, political economy, English literature, and chemistry.[16]

President Cravath wrote a recommendation commenting on DuBois's "unusually quick and active mind." Professor Chase remarked that DuBois might have given the impression of being conceited, yet it was not a trait "that would prevent his faithful work." Young DuBois was remembered by other instructors as honest, ambitious, diligent, and an excellent orator and writer.[17]

There is no doubt, Will DuBois got a first-rate education at Fisk. Forty years later when presenting a commencement address at his alma mater, he said his three years at Fisk had been an inspiration and had been spent in "nearly perfect happiness." With typical DuBois humor, he wrote at another time: "I think that my long years of life are due perhaps to one thing that I learned at Fisk, and that was to go to bed at ten o'clock at night."[18]

Will graduated from Fisk in 1888. He applied for and was given a $300 Price-Greenleaf scholarship to study for an advanced degree at Harvard University. After three years' absence he was going back home, but life for him would never be the same. It was just a matter of time before the love of his people would lure him back "down home" again.

# three

## I AM THE
## DARKER BROTHER

Deciding to attend Harvard was not something new to DuBois. He wrote, "I had always thought as a boy, that I was going to Harvard." Even though attending Fisk had been an excellent experience for him, he had been disappointed when he'd not been encouraged to attend Harvard for undergraduate study.[19]

In the late 1880s Harvard was the oldest and one of the most prestigious schools in the country. The Massachusetts Colony set aside 400 British pounds in 1636 to start a "Schoale or colledge" in Newetowne. The following year the township's name was changed to Cambridge in memory of the English college where about seventy Bostonian leaders had graduated. John Harvard, a Puritan minister, left an additional 750 British pounds and 260 books to the "wilderness school," and the college was officially named Harvard College in 1639. The charter dedicated the college to "the advancement of all good literature, arts, and sciences, and the education of English and Indian youth . . . in knowledge and godliness."[20]

Because of its open admittance policy, many people thought of Harvard as the stronghold of liberalism. Segregation was not practiced, so blacks were allowed to attend even when other institutions were closed to them. DuBois wrote in his autobiography that "Harvard was in an exceptional state of being at that time. I do not think that from 1885 to this day, there has been quite an aggregation of teachers and preachers and lecturers as there were then."

The question upon entering Harvard was: What career should he pursue? Poet? Philosopher? Journalist? Minister? Fisk president Cravath had encouraged DuBois to study for the ministry. But, Will was more interested in philosophy. "I wanted to study the thought of what *was*, the meaning to the whole universe," he wrote. Although he wasn't sure what his profession would be, DuBois knew that the purpose of his work would have but one motive: "to improve the condition of the race as a whole."[21]

At Harvard he repeated his junior and senior undergraduate years, with the bulk of his work in philosophy. Studying under some of the best minds of that day was a rare opportunity for any student regardless of race or creed.

William James and George Santayana were singled out as the two most important professors in this stage of DuBois's education. "My closest friend, for instance, as a teacher, was William James, the great sociologist, brother of Henry James. I knew him well; I was invited to his house and we talked together. Then there was George Santayana. He and I read the *Kritik der Reinen Vernuft* together, alone up in an attic room."[22]

George Santayana, then age twenty-six, was a highly respected Harvard professor, a Spanish-born American philosopher who would later be recog-

RVARD COLLEGE YARD
CAMBRIDGE, MASS.

Archival photo of Harvard College,
where DuBois completed his
undergraduate education and commenced
graduate studies. In 1896,
DuBois received a doctorate in
history and sociology from Harvard.

nized as a poet, novelist, and literary critic. Santayana's views were shaped by the classic philoso-
phers—Plato and Aristotle—yet his philosophic
skepticism and materialism were evident in his writings.

William James had been teaching at Harvard
since 1872. He was a pragmatist who viewed the
world as a "compromise between the objectively
given (the way things are) and the personally desired
(the way we wish things were)." James argued the
"ultimate test for us of what a truth means is the
conduct it dictates or inspires." He urged his students "to look for concreteness and facts, action and
power" in all thought.[23]

It was James, however, who finally convinced
DuBois to change his major to history. Philosophy
was an excellent field of study, but it was hard to
make a living practicing philosophy.

DuBois was a student at Harvard, but he never
really felt a part of it. Broderick states that Will
thought of the school as a "library and a faculty,
nothing more." He rented rooms on Flagg Street,
about a ten minute walk away, but except for attending class, he didn't participate in any school activities. "I never felt myself a Harvard man . . . If
they wanted to know me, the effort would have to
be on their part. Out of a class of three hundred, I
don't suppose that I knew ten really, intimately at
all."[24]

There were blacks who lived in Boston, and
DuBois knew them. In his autobiography, he wrote:
". . . there were colored people in Massachusetts,
and I had a pleasant social life with them so I was
not lonely at all and I enjoyed life there."[25]

That may have been true for a while, but DuBois grew impatient with the black community, and they grew weary of him. To help with the high cost of his education, DuBois gave lectures at local churches for a twenty-five-cent fee. A speech he gave during this time answered the argument some blacks were using to diminish the importance of education in relation to common sense, also known as "motherwit." In the opinions of some, education was snobbish, irreligious, and too expensive.

To DuBois, the accusation that scholars were snobs was just "so much fol-de-rol" (foolishness). He argued that no truly educated person would be guilty of snobbery, and that because a person chose not to associate with those with whom he had nothing in common, was not at all snobbery, but rather, social preference. In response to the charge that education was irreligious, he responded: "If religion won't stand the application of reason and common sense then it is not fit for the intelligent dog." This of course, did not sit well with Boston's conservative black clergy. DuBois even shared his own personal records to prove that an industrious person could get an education without a lot of money. Herewith, he presented his personal budget for the school year:

INCOME

| | |
|---|---|
| Summer Work | $125 |
| Scholarship | $200 |
| Tutoring | $50 |
| Monitorships | $10 |
| Prizes | $45 |
| TOTAL | $430 |

EXPENSES

| | |
|---|---|
| Tuition | $150 |
| Books | $25 |
| Room | $22 |
| Board (food) | $114 |
| Fuel, light | $11 |
| Clothing | $60 |
| Washing | $18 |
| Sundries | $30 |
| TOTAL | $430[26] |

Perhaps it was the tone of his delivery that turned the Boston audiences away. For example: It is generally accepted that leaders don't tell; they show. DuBois's early speeches were full of "telling." Armed with statistics and facts, he pointed out didactically that the black community enjoyed recreation and spent an estimated $5,000 a year on amusements. He then went on to outline a better program, more suitable because it included libraries, lectures, and literary societies.

In another speech, young DuBois complained that by condemning dancing and card-playing as sinful, churches drove youth into "less reputable places." He *told* the black community that what they ought to do was "put their money into an amusement center which would provide cultural uplift and still have a surplus to support some students at Harvard."

From early childhood, DuBois had been impatient with ignorance. In his zeal to share his knowledge, young DuBois often left behind those he was trying hardest to lead. His assertiveness, although well-intentioned, was often misunderstood as pushy. And soon, "Arrogant," "pompous," and "over-bearing" prefaced his name.[27]

Fortunately he was open to any learning experience. The speaking engagements proved to be an invaluable learning experience beyond any course work that he might have gotten at Harvard. He realized that knowledge alone did not make a leader. It would be by combining his knowledge and his passion for the race that he, W.E.B. DuBois, would one day take his place as one of the most persuasive speakers in the world. But while at Harvard he was still developing, learning, growing.

W.E.B. graduated from Harvard *cum laude*, 1890. The grades he earned for his second bachelors degree were exemplary A's, Bs, and only one C (in English composition). As one of six commencement speakers, he chose as his subject, "Jefferson Davis as a Representative of Civilization." (Jefferson Davis had been the president of the Confederate States during the Civil War.) The *Nation* praised DuBois, saying he handled the "hazardous subject with absolute good taste, great moderation, and almost contemptuous fairness."[28]

DuBois wrote later, "I tried to be very fair and frank in discussing the kind of civilization that he [Davis] represented—the might of the white race oppressing the rest of the world, which was a thing that we did not need and would not want in the next century." Indeed, he was learning to be persuasive without being abrasive.

Immediately following his graduation, DuBois applied for and received a grant for graduate work at Harvard. He studied for two more years, and then applied for a grant to study in Berlin, Germany. The way in which DuBois got his grant from the Slater

Fund is an interesting story he recorded in his autobiography:

At that time, Rutherford B. Hayes was head of the Slater Fund, which was based on money left by a Connecticut millionaire to educate Negroes, but Hayes said they had only been able to find orators. Well, I got angry at that, and I wrote Mr. Hayes and told him that I could get some professors to tell him that I was doing pretty good work and that I should like to study in Germany. That was at the time when every American who wanted to get a real position in a University had to go to Germany to get his degree.

Mr. Hayes wrote back politely and said that the Fund had offered some money for scholarships for Negroes, but that they were not being offered then. Following this, I wrote him a pretty impudent letter and said that he owed somebody an apology. He had no business going down to southern universities and speaking about a scholarship being offered, but not being able to find anybody. As a matter of fact, I had never heard of any such scholarship being offered, and I could not find out from any one else that they had heard. Well, Mr. Hayes wrote a very apologetic letter and said that he was sorry and would take up the matter the very next year, if I wished. The next year, I started on him again, and I got everybody from the President of Harvard on down, to write. He was simply overwhelmed with recommendations. I got a fellowship. Meanwhile, I had gotten a renewal on my fellowship, so that I spent two years in the Harvard Graduate School. Then I got the fellowship to Germany. It was $750, half of it a gift and half was to be paid back after I had finished my education. I eventually paid it back with interest at 6 percent.[29]

After receiving his master's degree from Harvard in 1892, DuBois went to Germany to study for his doctorate at the University of Berlin.

When DuBois arrived in Europe, imperialism was at its peak. The economic, cultural, political, religious, and physical domination of one people over another was led by Great Britain. Although other European countries joined in the scramble for colonies, the British Empire acquired up to a third of its colonies during the eleven years between 1879 and 1890.

Asia and the Middle East were carved up between the major powers, but the most tragic victim of imperialism was the continent of Africa. At the Berlin-Africa Conference of 1885, sixteen European participants had sliced up the continent. Only two countries on the continent remained independent: Liberia, founded by former American slaves, and Ethiopia.

Germany, under the leadership of Prime Minister Otto Von Bismarck, had rejected the concept of imperialism, choosing instead industrial expansion at home. Bismarck was a powerful leader, but Emperor William II proved to be more powerful. In 1890, Bismarck was dismissed. Germany still did not, however, become a major imperialist force.

DuBois arrived in Germany at a time when great scientific concepts such as thermodynamics and electrochemistry were advancing civilization by quantum leaps. Marie and Pierre Curie had investigated uranium and discovered polonium and radium. Lister had made surgery safe, and Pasteur had developed the "germ theory" of disease. Sigmund Freud's work in "psychoanalysis" was a "new science that rectified the psyche's aberrations." People were living longer and better lives.

Right away Will knew that getting away from the states and the constant nagging of race relations would be good for him. He felt as though he'd been carrying the entire race on his shoulders. In Berlin, race didn't seem to matter.

He spoke fluent German so communication was not a problem. He went to the theater weekly, and traveled as far as his meager budget would allow. A German family took him under their wing. In the beer halls where students gathered, he was welcomed. If his color was mentioned, it was done so out of genuine curiosity and not for meanness or spite. He was the darker brother, but still a brother, no less loved by his fellow man. It was a joy to live without having to worry about race.

Meanwhile, DuBois sent letters back home to black newspapers. And, once again, he was attacked for telling about his personal experiences. His enthusiasm was criticized by some for being too self-centered. The *Cleveland Gazette* commented: "Much of W.E.B. DuBois's letters from Europe published in the New York *Age* make me tired. 'I, I, I, I, Me, me, me. Black bread and butter,' *Scat!*"[30]

Although he enjoyed living in Europe and it would have been easy to slip into an endless holiday,

DuBois knew the rigor required to earn a doctorate. And, as always, he was diligent in his research and study.

The bulk of his days were spent studying under Gustav Schmoller, concluding this seminar with a research paper entitled: "The Plantation and Peasant Proprietorship Systems of Agriculture in the Southern United States." The paper was so well done, Professor Schmoller wanted to publish it in the yearbook.

Still, his Berlin term ended in disappointment. Although University of Berlin records show that his work was outstanding, Will was not allowed to take the final examinations that would qualify him for a doctorate degree. "You had to have been there three semesters . . . and I had only been two, because I only had money for two. They tried to make an exception, but the English professor had a lot of candidates, so that no difference could be made. I brought to their attention the fact that I had already had two years at Harvard, but they did not recognize Harvard as being of the same rank as Berlin."

DuBois came back to America without a doctorate from Berlin. In 1958, while lecturing in Berlin, the university brought out his records and awarded him the doctorate they had denied him seventy years before.

DuBois had known for a long time what his life's work would be, and he had spent years preparing himself for the job. As a teacher and researcher, he planned to work on his theory that *if white men were prejudiced because of ignorance, and black men were held back because of their ignorance, then education had to be the key to reconciling the races.*

By that time he had abandoned philosophy as a

career, but his approach to history and sociology were rooted in the philosophical search for Truth. On New Year's Eve, while still a student in Germany, DuBois had written in his diary "The Universe is Truth. The Best ought to be. On these postulates hang all the law and the prophets."[31]

# four

## THE MISSION: TO TRAIN
## THE TALENTED TENTH

DuBois's education was not complete until 1896, when he received a doctorate in history and sociology from Harvard. However, he accepted a position as chairman of the department of classics at Wilberforce University at Xenia, Ohio, in 1894. Wilberforce was an all-black school sponsored by the African Methodist Episcopal Church.

The A.M.E. Church, founded by Richard Allen in 1787, is the oldest African-American institution in existence. Allen rebelled against racial restrictions imposed on black members of St. George's Methodist Church in Philadelphia. In protest, Allen left St. George's Church and organized a new denomination. Wilberforce was a university developed from this proud tradition and heritage that Dr. DuBois entered in the summer of 1894. The university felt privileged to have him on staff, for very few black men had his qualifications. [32]

Filled with enthusiasm, DuBois traveled to Ohio. His Vandyke beard, tall silk hat, gloves, and cane gave him a look of "severe elegance." There was always a sense of urgency in his manner. He walked with purpose and spoke quickly. For a while DuBois considered himself "half-happy." But in a short time, he became wholly unhappy with the school's rigid social restraints.

For example, separate paths were provided so that even a casual meeting could not take place between male and female students. Attendance at Sunday school and revivals was "required." DuBois could not logically connect academic success with religious piety, so it wasn't long before he was in trouble with the school's administration. Within two years he left Wilberforce.

The bright spot in his stay in Ohio was Nina Gomer, a young student from Cedar Rapids, Iowa, whom he married. She was described as a beautiful young woman with large, dark eyes and a shy smile.

At the end of his second term in Ohio, he was appointed by the University of Pennsylvania to write a scholarly paper about black Philadelphians. It was a fifteen-month assignment that paid only $60 a month, but he took it to get away from Wilberforce.

Nina went with her husband to Philadelphia where they lived in small, cramped slum quarters. The young bride was frequently left alone, for her husband was totally absorbed by his work. Rather than complain, which she knew would do no good, Nina DuBois busied herself with projects that made their home more comfortable when they were together. It was not ideal, but the DuBoises were happy.[33]

The work Will produced during this period was incredible. While he was in Philadelphia, his dissertation from Harvard was published, entitled: "The Suppression of the African Slave-Trade to the United States of America, 1639 to 1870."

DuBois's view was "the slave trade could have been curtailed by three methods: by raising moral standards, by enforcing legal prohibition of the slave trade, or by destroying the economic attractions of the traffic in men." It was difficult for DuBois to remain objective in this paper, perhaps it was because he was black, and writing about slavery was too sensitive an issue for him to treat with total objectivity. Some critics attacked his exhortative language, for example, "It behooves nations as well as men to do things at the very moment when they ought to be done." Yet, the thesis earned him a Harvard Ph.D. and recognition among contemporary scholars.[34]

The culmination of his work at the University of Pennsylvania resulted in another excellent document: "The Philadelphia Negro, A Social Study." In this work, DuBois advanced his theory that education could be the salvation of African-Americans. He stated that "the first impulse of the best, the wisest, and richest is to segregate themselves from the mass." DuBois warned that this would not help elevate the race, for no matter how "laudable an ambition to rise may be, the first duty of an upper class is to serve the lowest classes."

At the foundation of Dr. DuBois's theory was the "talented tenth" philosophy. One of his biographers, Jack B. Moore, describes the concept as "the successful Negroes whose duty he felt was to employ their position and resources to help raise the masses left behind at the bottom of the American ladder of prosperity." Another biographer, Francis Broderick, put it, ". . . like all races, DuBois said, the Negro race would be saved by its exceptional men . . . as teachers, ministers, professional men, spokesmen, the exceptional few," that is, the "talented tenth" had to emerge as leaders.[35]

Shortly after arriving in Philadelphia, Atlanta University's president, Horace Bumstead, invited DuBois to join the sociology department faculty. DuBois was apprehensive about accepting the appointment because Atlanta University also had a religious affiliation. But, Bumstead was an unusual administrator who made allowances for DuBois's personal beliefs.

W.E.B. returned to the South, arriving in Atlanta in 1897. He remained there for thirteen years.

Nina was pregnant at the time, so he sent her to the Burghardts in Great Barrington. There, their son, Burghardt DuBois was born in 1898. DuBois expressed his feelings about becoming a father:

What is this tiny formless thing, this newborn wail from an unknown world—all head and voice? I handle it curiously, and watch perplexed its winking, breathing, and sneezing. I did not love it then; it seemed a ludicrous thing to love; but, her I loved my girl-mother, she whom I now saw unfolding like the glory of the morning . . . Through her I came to love the wee thing . . . So sturdy and masterful he grew, so filled with bubbling life.[36]

It was a happy time. He had a new job, a wife he loved, and a beautiful new baby. Everything was in place for him to begin his work, which he attacked with a zealot's fury.

Berlin University professor Schmoller was a great influence on his early Atlanta work, which was moving more toward sociology than history. DuBois's primary goal was to prepare the "talented tenth"—those college students who would one day become the leaders of the race. He assigned himself three tasks, described by biographer Broderick as: "to assemble accurate sociological data as the basis of intelligent social policy toward the Negro; to present the Negro's problems in a favorable light to a larger nonscholarly audience through lectures, books and magazine articles; to take the lead in bringing culture to American Negroes."

But even the best laid plans don't always work out the way the planner designs them. Tragedy entered the DuBois home when, at eighteen months, little Burghardt died. In his essay, "Of the passing of the First-Born," the bereaved father described his sorrow:

> He died at eventide, when the sun lay like a brooding sorrow above the western hills, veiling its face; when the winds spoke not, and the trees, the great green trees he loved, stood motionless. I saw his breath beat quicker, and quicker, pause and then his little soul leapt like a star that travels in the night and left a world of darkness in its train . . . Well sped, my boy, before the world has dubbed your ambition insolence, has held your ideals unattainable, and taught you to cringe and bow. Better for this nameless void that stops my life than a sea of sorrow for you.[37]

Nina mourned the loss of her son the rest of her life, and though she would smile again, there was always a corner of sorrow in her heart where gladness could not penetrate. Sixteen months after the

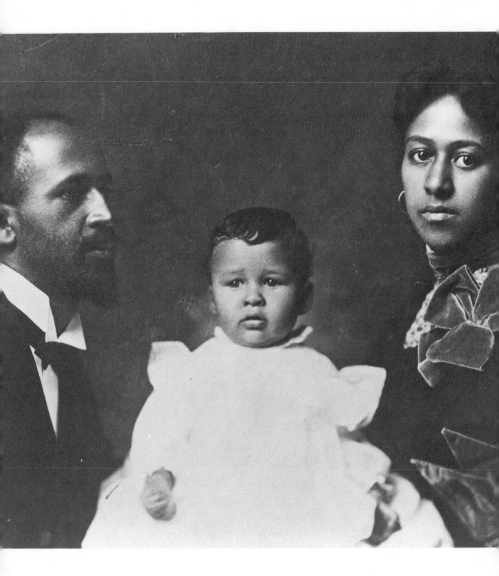

*Left to right: DuBois,
his daughter Yolande,
and his wife Nina.*

death of Burghardt, daughter Nina Yolande was born. They called her Yolande. The baby gave her mother a reason for living and her father someone to spoil and adore. Burghardt was forever missed but no child could have been more cherished than Yolande DuBois.

Meanwhile, a century was coming to a close. Thirty-five years had passed since the Civil War ended. Passage of the Fourteenth, Fifteenth, and Sixteenth Amendments should have safeguarded the Constitutional rights of all Americans, but that was not happening.

Human rights were at an all-time low in America by the 1900s. In order to reunify itself, the country fought and defeated the native Americans, forcing them onto reservations, thus freeing western lands for settlement. East Coast industries were booming, but there were no child labor laws to protect young children who worked in unsafe environments; there were no federal safety regulations, no health benefits nor retirement benefits for workers. All efforts by workers to unionize were met with hostility. Women couldn't vote or hold public office. Asian and Mexican immigration was discouraged and even limited by federal restrictions. And, in America's southland, African-Americans were trapped in an endless cycle of racism and discrimination.

For all practical purposes, Reconstruction ended in 1876, when, as a part of a political pay-off, President Rutherford B. Hayes pulled federal troops out of the South, and then made a goodwill tour of the region. These actions sent a signal that the rebels were forgiven. Soon southerners were again being appointed to key political positions, including to the

United States Supreme Court. Supreme Court Justices are not supposed to allow personal prejudices to interfere with their decisions. Unfortunately, beginning in the 1880s, racism did affect the decisions of the court.

State laws, in clear violation of the Constitution, were upheld; loopholes were found to support the cases. In various states, blacks were losing the right to serve on juries, own property, use public facilities, receive a fair trial, and to vote. Meanwhile, a majority of the legal guardians of the Constitution looked the other way.

Homer Plessy, a black passenger, was denied a first-class seat on a Louisiana train although he had purchased a ticket. There were plenty of seats available, but he was forced to ride in a separate car provided for blacks only. The case was taken to the Supreme Court. In the infamous *Plessy* v. *Ferguson* decision of 1896, the court ruled that "separate but equal" was constitutionally acceptable. It was reasoned that since both the black and white cars were described as equal in all ways, then the fact that they were separate did not matter. The majority opinion ruled that the Fourteenth Amendment was not intended to "abolish distinctions based on color, or to enforce social equality as distinguished from political equality or a commingling of the two races upon terms unsatisfactory to either."[38]

Justice John Marshall Harlan, who wrote the court's only dissenting opinion, warned that the decision would allow states to "interfere with the full enjoyment of the blessings of freedom; to regulate civil rights common to all citizens, upon the basis of race; and to place in a condition of legal inferiority a large body of American citizens."

Justice Harlan was correct. Within the year, the United States was a nation divided along color lines. Race riots and lynchings stirred up old resentments and formed new reasons to hate. In April 1899, white and black workers clashed over jobs in Pana, Illinois, and six persons were killed. Although black soldiers had valiantly faced death on foreign soil in the Spanish-American War, eighty-five of their brothers were reportedly lynched in December 1899.[39]

The social and political upheaval at the turn of the century directly affected W.E.B. DuBois's work as both a teacher and researcher. More than ever he believed that the education of the "talented tenth" was paramount for racial improvement.

As a parent, he was also concerned about the changing and hostile southern environment. While attending Fisk, DuBois had avoided making trips outside the university to keep from having to deal with racism. He would not permit his daughter to go beyond the grounds of Atlanta University for the same reason. He feared that she might be psychologically harmed by a racist encounter. In no way did he want his daughter to feel inferior to anyone.

During the summer, Yolande was sent away to New England where she was exposed to cultural activities unavailable to southern black children of that day.

W.E.B. DuBois might have been content to work and study in his ivy-towered environment, fighting racism among academicians, if it had not been for the rise of one man—Booker T. Washington.

# five

## W.E.B. AND BOOKER T.

The faculty and administration at Atlanta University was practically all white, while the student body was all black. It was an arrangement with which DuBois was familiar if not altogether comfortable.

He lived in a cloistered environment on the campus of the University, leaving only to do necessary shopping. He rarely rode a streetcar, went to a concert or a theater, and when in public, he was always formal and academic.

When white staff members wanted to visit him, they had to seek him out in his study. Because of Dr. DuBois's serious and restrained manner, many people—both blacks and whites—thought he was a difficult man, hard to know, and a bit too serious.

But there was another side to the man, a side he reserved for his wife and daughter, close friends and associates. Those who were closest to him knew he was incredibly shy and careful about showing affection for fear of rejection. One friend described him as sincere, devoted, fun-loving, even comical.

Nina DuBois was neither an outgoing nor an outspoken person. She worked hard at helping make the DuBois home a warm and inviting place where visitors felt welcomed. The house was neat and attractively decorated, an ideal meeting place. Dr. DuBois's private library was a scholar's dream, and his books and papers were open to industrious students and dedicated colleagues.[40]

Once a month, a gathering of local black college professors assembled at the DuBois home. They discussed art, music, drama, science and literature in an open, relaxed manner. At these times, DuBois was at ease, and took a breather from the feeling that he carried the whole race on his shoulders. However, the "race problem" was a topic that was frequently discussed. At the turn of the century, one of the most controversial persons of the day was Booker Taliaferro Washington.

The controversy had begun in 1895 when Booker T. Washington delivered a speech at the Cotton Exposition in which he seemingly accepted second-class citizenship for blacks, and approved segregation of the races.

In September 1895, DuBois's first year at Atlanta University, Booker T. Washington was asked to speak at the Atlanta Exposition. Southerners who came to hear the Alabama educator wondered what he might say. Would he talk about the lynchings of innocent men and women at the hands of lawless individuals who refused to obey Constitutional law? Would he point out the injustices of voting rights violations occurring all over the South? Would he call to everyone's attention the unsatisfactory conditions of black housing and education? While the white crowd nervously anticipated what the speaker might say, the black population stood by proudly and hopefully. For some blacks the content of Washington's speech didn't matter. That he had

Booker T. Washington (1856–1915),
founder and head of the
Tuskegee Institute in Tuskegee,
Alabama. In Souls of Black Folk,
DuBois wrote a stinging polemic
against Washington's advice to
blacks to "cast your buckets
down where you are."

been invited by the southern white establishment was satisfaction enough.

On that bright September day, Washington presented himself well. Described by one newspaper reporter as "a remarkable figure; tall, bony, straight as a Sioux chief, high forehead, straight nose, heavy jaws, and strong, determined mouth, with bright white teeth, and piercing eyes and a commanding manner . . .," he stood before the sea of white faces.[41]

Booker T., the former slave, began by apologizing for his race, saying they were wrong for wanting to begin "at the top" of the social ladder rather than "at the bottom." In Washington's opinion, his brethren were wrong for wanting to be leaders instead of accepting the jobs that were available to them as house servants and laborers.

Using an analogy, Washington described the captains of two ships coming together at the mouth of the Amazon River. One captain called out for fresh water. The other captain answered, "Cast your buckets down where you are." Three times, there was a call for fresh water, and three times the same response was given. "Cast your buckets down where you are."

The narrator then explained what both races could learn from his story. He suggested that people of color should *cast their buckets down where they were* by using the skills they'd learned best in slavery—housekeeping, cooking, farming, and manual labor. To whites he suggested that they, too, should *cast their buckets down where they were* by hiring the thousands of southern blacks who were "among the most patient, faithful, law-abiding, and unresentful people that the world had ever seen."

Washington finished by offering a "compromise," saying, "the wisest among my race understand that the agitation of questions of social equality is the extremest error and that progress in the employment of all the privileges that will come to us must be the result of severe and constant struggles rather than artificial forcing." At this point the speaker held up his hand and spread his fingers apart. He continued: "In all things that are social, we can be as separate as the fingers . . ." Then making a fist, he concluded, "yet, one as the hand in all things essential for mutual progress."[42]

The white crowd cheered and applauded wildly, tossing long-standing racial customs in the air along with their hats and bonnets. For example, Georgia's governor shook Washington's hand, something that was not done at that time, and certainly not in public. And, an astonished newspaper reporter wrote: "the fairest women of Georgia stood up and cheered."

Thereafter, white political leadership proclaimed Booker T. Washington the spokesman for *all* African-Americans. Not all African-Americans, however, had agreed with the speech that would become known as "the Atlanta Compromise." But no other person would be more persistent in his opposition to Washington's suggestion that blacks accept segregation and second-class citizenship than W.E.B. DuBois.

Charting the conflict between DuBois and Washington is complicated. It does help, however, to understand the different backgrounds which shaped their attitudes.

Both men possessed monumental egos with ambitions to match. DuBois was born in the east, the great-grandson of men who had known no master. He was sure of his ability because he had never been limited. Born a slave in 1856, Washington understood what it meant to be owned like a dog and sold like a horse, yet he had still managed to achieve in spite of these seemingly insurmountable limitations.[43]

Young Will had enjoyed playing pretend war in Great Barrington, but Booker T. endured the perils of a real war and had survived hunger and disease. While still a teenager, Will DuBois had more education than some men twice his age. He wrote articles for a New York newspaper, won debates, and performed in plays. Success helped make him an achiever. According to his biographer, Louis Harlan, Booker T. was forced from childhood "to deceive . . . to wear the mask." His achievements grew out of adversity.

DuBois felt superior to poor white factory workers who migrated into Great Barrington looking for work. Washington understood firsthand the power one man could hold over another simply because of skin color.

As a student in the United States and Germany, DuBois learned by thinking; he grew up believing knowledge was the best weapon against ignorance and an essential tool black men and women needed to build the future. That is why he had become a teacher.

Washington learned by doing. Hard physical work was the foundation upon which he built his life. At the time he was working in a West Virginia coal mine, he also walked and begged rides "both in wagons and in the [train] cars, traveling five-hundred miles to Hampton Normal College in

Hampton, Virginia," where, in 1875 he earned what is today equivalent to a high school diploma. Washington believed hard work was the key to individual and racial success. That is why he became a teacher.

In 1881, when DuBois was only thirteen, Washington, at age twenty-five, was asked to become the principal of Tuskegee Normal Institute, Tuskegee, Alabama. He accepted. The school was little more than a shack and a rickety church building. Through his hard work it became a leading educational institution which still stands today.

While DuBois was learning how to think at Fisk, Harvard and Berlin, Booker T. Washington was teaching his Tuskegee students, many of whom were former slaves, how to achieve by using their hands. By mastering bricklaying, carpentry, furniture making, and other industrial crafts, Washington believed he was building men of character. He used his own rise from poverty and degradation as an example of what was possible. He was a powerful role model.

But in time DuBois became a role model, too, challenging his students to think, to reason, and to challenge ignorance with research and facts.

Clearly, the life experiences of each man was reflected in his philosophy regarding the handling of the "race problem" as it existed in the first decade of the 1900s. DuBois believed the "talented tenth" would join with whites and lead both races to a better understanding of one another. Washington's solution was the complete opposite. He believed that by imitating white standards and accepting white values, his people would "earn" white people's respect and friendship, and thus ensure racial harmony. The goal at Tuskegee was "to turn out graduates who were successful farmers, carpenters, and bricklayers. . .sober, hardworking citizens who minded their own business."

After the Atlanta Exposition, Washington became a much sought-after speaker among whites. The substance of his presentations were similar in content and tone to the "Compromise." Though Washington's intent was not to relegate his own people to second-class citizenship, there is no doubt, his finger-fist analogy gave segregationalists a rationale for the "separate but equal" legal loophole they were using to undermine Constitutional law.

Southern whites and northern philanthropists liked Washington's nondemanding, nonthreatening approach, his quiet conciliatory language. Soon he became the designated spokesman for "Colored America," and support for Tuskegee grew.

The Alabama patriarch ruled "Colored America"—a term used by whites to limit and define the power and scope of a black leader—from his Tuskegee stronghold—sometimes mockingly called "the black White House." He bore his burdens like a beleaguered father, weary from battling with his large and unruly family. As his biographer Louis Harlan noted, Washington knew how "to play roles, wear the mask, depending upon the group he was addressing." Although he never lashed out at his opponents publicly, it has been reported he said plenty in private.

It is interesting to note that DuBois's opposition to Washington's position was not immediate. He wasn't counted among the early opponents. Based on his training in childhood, it was hard to argue with Washington's catchwords like "self-help," "honesty," "hard work," "thrift," and "discipline."

These were the virtues all men, regardless of color, valued. The two men held some measure of respect for each other. Washington had, in fact, invited DuBois to join the Tuskegee faculty, but Will had already accepted the position at Atlanta University by the time the letter had arrived.

While DuBois privately questioned some of Washington's social, economic, and educational positions, and doubted if his course was the best path for race improvement, Dr. DuBois carefully avoided any public confrontation, finding praiseworthy things to say instead. In his opinion, it was not wise for black leaders to air their differences in public, where even good, honest debate might undermine their efforts.

Also, at the time, DuBois didn't see himself as a leader but rather in the more important role of teacher of leaders. In the five years from 1895 to 1900 DuBois was happily immersed in his research.

By degrees, however, the relationship between the two men grew strained. Even when Washington saw blacks losing the right to vote and other civil rights, he still counseled his people to forget about political and social equality—work hard and things would get better—one day.

DuBois was furious; still he kept his peace. Other black leaders were very articulate in their anti-Washington sentiments. Charles W. Chesnutt, the novelist, Ida Wells Barnett, chairman of the Anti-Lynching League; educator Kelly Miller; and Monroe Trotter, editor of the *Boston Guardian* were the most active voices.

Monroe Trotter, also a Harvard graduate, was jailed when he challenged Washington during a speech in Boston 1903. Washington's supporters, who were, for the most part, white and powerful, led a counterattack suggesting that Trotter and other critics were troublemakers, malcontents, radicals, and much worse, jealous-hearted and mean-spirited.

Trying to be fair, DuBois admonished Trotter, too, for his violent verbal attack on the Alabama educator, but Washington's overreaction to criticism was also noted. In private, Dr. DuBois was troubled by the implication that somehow it was "unsafe" to confront Washington. DuBois knew how the "Tuskegee Machine" operated. It was a powerful force to challenge. Any and all opposition was quietly but systematically crushed. All matters that concerned black people were sent by white philanthropists to Booker T. Washington for his stamp of approval. Without it, no grants were given, no funds were dispersed. Those who agreed with Washington were rewarded with measured opportunity; those who disagreed were simply "forgotten."[44]

DuBois had remained relatively subdued until the Trotter jailing, then he decided black people wanted and needed another leadership option. He was reluctant to "take on Tuskegee." To him, racism and discrimination were the real enemies. If, however, what he had to say against injustice was misunderstood as a personal attack on Washington, then in that respect, he was ready to "take on Tuskegee."

If the conflict between Booker T. and W.E.B. can be described as a battle, then DuBois's choice of weapons was the pen. His attack was launched in a book of essays titled *The Souls of Black Folk*, a literary classic, an American treasure.

# six

## THE SOULS OF
## BLACK FOLK

DuBois declared philosophical war against Booker
T. Washington in *The Souls of Black Folk* published
in 1903, and in so doing, offered black people an
alternative leader.

*The Souls of Black Folk* contains fourteen essays
in which he described "the spiritual world in which
ten thousand thousand Americans live and strive."
In the first two chapters he showed what freedom
finally meant to the African-American and what had
happened since the emancipation. In subsequent
chapters he explained his concept of education, the
struggles of the "black peasantry" and ended with a
look at the souls of black folk—the meaning of their
religion, the passion of their human sorrow, and the
struggle of their collective soul.

The book was an instant best-seller. And while
it covered a wide range of materials, some of which
had been published before, it was chapter three that
caused the stir within literary and political circles.
In the "Forethought," DuBois stated, "In a third
chapter, I have tried to show the slow rise of personal
leadership, and criticized candidly the leader who
bears the chief burden of his race today."

In the beginning of "Of Mr. Booker T. Washington and Others," DuBois set the lure for his readers. He began by praising Washington. Then he restated Booker T.'s position, clearly and concisely. Washington wanted blacks to postpone until some indefinite time three important things: political power, civil rights, and higher education of youth.

Then, by contrast, Dr. DuBois summarized the occurrences following Washington's "Atlanta Compromise" (1895 to 1903): "The disfranchisement of the Negro, the legal creation of a distinct status of civil inferiority, and the steady withdrawal of aid from institutions for the higher training of the Negro." While DuBois didn't blame Washington for all these developments, he did say, "his propaganda has, without a shadow of doubt helped their speedier accomplishment."

As the reader moves into the essay, the language gets stronger and stronger. DuBois uses a question, to which he already knows the answer, but to which he wants his readers to arrive at on their own. "Is it possible, and probable, that nine millions of men can make effective progress in economic lines if they are deprived of political rights, made a servile caste, and allowed only the most meager chance for developing their exceptional men?" The reader is ready to respond along with DuBois: "No!"

DuBois argues that "Mr. Washington thus faces the triple paradox of his career." He lists them:

1. He is striving nobly to make Negro artisans business men and property-owners; but it is utterly impossible, under modern competitive methods, for workingmen and property-owners to defend their rights and exist without the right of suffrage.

(62)

2. He insists on thrift and self-respect, but at the same time counsels a silent submission to civic inferiority such as is bound to sap the manhood of any race in the long run.

3. He advocates common-school and industrial training, and deprecates institutions of higher learning; but neither the Negro common-schools, nor Tuskegee itself, could remain open a day were it not for teachers trained in Negro colleges, or trained by their graduates.

On this last point DuBois noted the fact that Washington had invited him to join the Tuskegee staff . . ."name your price" was the offer. Of course he had declined.

Throughout the essay, DuBois writes like a boxer—blocking with his right hand and jabbing with his left. In one paragraph, DuBois shields himself behind praises for Washington, only to level a swift and hard-hitting critical blow in the next. For example, DuBois writes:

It would be unjust to Mr. Washington not to acknowledge that in several instances he has opposed movements in the South which were unjust to the Negro . . . Notwithstanding this, it is equally true to assert that on the whole the distinct impression left by Mr. Washington's propaganda is, first, that the South is justified in its present attitude toward the Negro because of the Negro's degradation; secondly, that the prime cause of the Negro's failure to rise more quickly is his wrong education in the past; and thirdly, that his future rise depends primarily on his own efforts. Each of these propositions is a dangerous half-truth.

By the conclusion of the Washington essay, DuBois calls for all blacks to take an open stand against "the compromiser," no matter how unpopular their positions might be. There could in his opinion be no justification or apologies for injustice.

DuBois would pay for his opposition to Washington. He was branded a militant, a maverick, a radical. Supporters rallied to Washington's defense, pointing out that DuBois was an academic pedant, who was jealous and petty. The DuBois camp defended him with equal fervor.

Washington's biographer Harlan suggests in defense of Washington, that DuBois and other men who had not had any dealings with slavery could not fully understand Washington's actions. "[His] ultimate plans for blacks were deeply hidden beneath the masks he donned at will in public, permitting him to preach separateness but covertly to attack . . . the radical settlement he publicly accepted, like a double agent who infiltrated the white power elite in order to subvert it—a Br'er Rabbit."

DuBois biographer Moore points out that it is more likely DuBois felt "toward the older and more established man . . . a certain ambivalence—such as a son might feel toward a father who had rejected him—seeing Washington, an authority figure who should give him guidance and recognition, but whom he would ultimately have to reject to establish himself."

Their motives have been the topic of many a

debate, poem, and lecture. The irony, of course, is that both men had the same goals, but they had different methods of achieving them. Neither leader had *the* answer to the race problems in America. African-Americans are too diverse for any one theory to be practical. And, it is ludicrous to believe that "one" spokesperson would be accepted by all black people. Much of the resistance to Washington's leadership was in defiance of the whites who "selected" him as "the black leader." DuBois was a welcomed option—another voice.

How did the conflict affect DuBois and his "life's work?" Being at the center of controversy was not altogether disagreeable to DuBois. He liked a good debate, especially when it was a topic he cared about. And once committed, he did not back down easily. For years he had sought support from Harvard and Columbia to advance the scientific study of racial conflict. Predictably, the funds dried up. The reason given: no need for "scientific work of this sort." Knowing that if he softened his tone, the funds might open up, DuBois still would not acquiesce.

All in all, the years 1895 to 1903 were a tremendous growing period for him. The haughty young man, who at age sixteen had advised the people of Great Barrington to check with him before selecting a book to read, had matured. A grant could mean a great deal to his work. Should he take the advice of some counselors and try to make amends with Washington?

Then, on one of those rare occasions when he ventured beyond the walls of Atlanta University to visit a friend, DuBois passed a grocery store. He stopped to look at a curious display in the window, which, much to his revulsion, turned out to be the knuckles of a black man who had been hanged and mutilated. Sickened to the point of nausea, he hurried home.

Never again would he be able to treat the race problem with cool, scientific detachment. He vowed to stand up for justice and never be silenced until his goal was achieved. For all practical purposes his work at Atlanta University had come to an end. It was time for him to climb down from the ivy-covered tower.[45]

# seven

## A RACE IN CRISIS

It was DuBois's militancy that stirred the souls of other well-educated, professional black men of the day. Filled with race pride and ready to act boldly, they championed DuBois as their leader. They were ready for his leadership and he was ready to lead them.

The Niagara Movement was the brainchild of DuBois. It was an organization that advocated the rights of black people, militant in tone, but nonviolent in its approach.

It began in 1905, when DuBois sent out a letter— some call it a summons—to black professionals all over the country. Hotels in Buffalo, New York refused accommodations to the group, so DuBois found a small Canadian hotel near Niagara Falls where the meeting could be held.

From July 11–13, 1905, twenty-nine black men met and formed an alliance to fight racism and discrimination in America. They issued what has been called a "stinging manifesto to white America." They vowed "to stand up for manhood rights, denounce and defeat oppressive laws, and assail the ears and the conscience of white Americans so long as America is unjust."

On January 31, 1906, fifty-nine men from seventeen states incorporated the organization and a Declaration of Principles was issued protesting lynching, the denial of the vote, segregated public facilities, poor schools, inadequate housing, unemployment, and underemployment. It didn't take long for the group to be labeled extremists.[46]

The next meeting, scheduled for the summer of 1906, was held at Harpers Ferry, the scene of the raid led by John Brown. John Brown was a hero among blacks. He led a raid on Harpers Ferry, Virginia, on October 16, 1859, with twenty-one men. His plan was to seize the arsenal and arm slaves in nearby plantations so they could fight for their own freedom. Brown was captured and hanged, but he became a martyr in the eyes of abolitionists.

The meeting at Harpers Ferry helped the organization subtly remind observers that the abolitionist movement worked because blacks and whites worked together to overcome slavery. To overcome segregation, it would again require cooperation between the races.

Meanwhile, shocking events destabilized race relations even more. Tension erupted into violence; on September 22–24, 1906, there was a race riot in Atlanta. Whites went into the black community and burned homes, beat innocent people, and murdered anybody who dared try to stop them. Martial law was proclaimed. Twelve people were killed before the violence finally ended. DuBois abhorred violence, but he secured a gun to protect his family from the mob.

The next month, three thousand blacks protested in Philadelphia against the performance of the stage play, *The Clansman*, by Thomas Dixon.

The play was an attempt to justify the existence of the Ku Klux Klan. That year sixty-two blacks were reported lynched, and not one single person was indicted, tried, or convicted of murder. This kind of senseless killing and violence continued throughout 1907.[47]

Along with two associates, in January 1907, DuBois founded the *Horizon,* a monthly journal. The magazine was not sponsored by any organization, however, the articles, mostly written by DuBois, strongly supported the Niagara Movement's positions and condemned the senseless killings and rioting.

DuBois ran *The Horizon* out of his office in Atlanta, but most of the time there wasn't enough money for paper and postage. One of his partners, L.M. Hershaw, owned a printing shop, so costs were held to a minimum. But, subscribers were few; advertisers were fewer still. Although the journal's articles were excellent, it was a financial disaster. To keep the publication going, the partners had to personally finance the operations.

Evidence shows that through DuBois's persistence, ideas did get out to the intellectual black community and to those whites who were interested in knowing the truth about the race situation. During the Harpers Ferry meeting it became evident that not only *The Horizon* was in financial difficulty, but the entire Niagara Movement.

Although there were close to four hundred members, the organization was $2,650 in debt. There was no central office for the organization, so committees were scattered all over the country. Although dues were lowered to help increase membership and raise revenue, the situation continued

Members of the Niagara
Movement, founded by
DuBois in 1905 to fight
racism and discrimination
in America. DuBois is
seated in the front
row on the left.

to worsen. Many southern blacks were especially frightened by white objections to the "radical" image.

Finally in 1908 at the Boston meeting, it was clear the Niagara Movement was crumbling. DuBois still clung to hope, and pleaded passionately for his colleagues to at least rally to keep the *Horizon* going.[48]

In December 1908, Jack Johnson defeated Tommy Burns in Sydney, Australia, for the heavyweight boxing championship. Another outbreak of violence followed. White supremacists were appalled by the notion that a black man could defeat a white man, even in a competitive sport like boxing. Johnson's win threatened the very foundation upon which white supremacy was structured—control by fear.

During the first decade of the twentieth century, there were 8,833,994 black Americans. Well over 80 percent of them lived in the rural South, where often they outnumbered whites by a three-to-one ratio. White control was maintained by using intimidation, ignorance, and fear; to keep blacks "in their place" they had to be "kept in line." And often that meant violence of the most heinous kind—like the Springfield, Illinois, riot of 1908.

In the birthplace of Abraham Lincoln, the "Great Emancipator," white mobs attacked and beat any black who crossed their path. They shouted, "Lincoln freed you, we'll show you your place." But the violence against blacks must have gone too far, because it mobilized white liberals against segregation and discrimination, in the fashion that resembled the abolitionists, who united against slavery in the 1850s.

In a response to the Springfield riots, William English Walling expressed his outrage in a newspaper editorial. "It is time," he said, "for the nation to take action." It wasn't an immediate or overwhelming movement, but a conference of both black and white leaders to discuss the social, political, and economic conditions of blacks in America was called on February 12, 1909. W.E.B. DuBois was invited and he accepted the invitation.

Out of that first meeting came a statement which outlined the problems facing blacks living in white-controlled America.

> In many states Lincoln would find justice enforced, if at all, by judges elected by one element in a community to pass upon the liberties and lives of another. He would see the black men and women, for whose freedom a hundred thousand soldiers gave their lives, set apart in trains, in which they pay first-class fares for third-class service, and segregated in railway stations and in places of entertainment; he would observe that State after State declines to do its elementary duty in preparing the Negro through education for the best exercises of citizenship. [49]

May 30, 1909, three hundred blacks and whites met in New York to continue laying the foundation of the new organization that would combine the efforts of both races.

Leading black "militants" were in attendance—Monroe Trotter, Ida Wells Barnett, J. Max Barber, and Mary Church Terrell. Still, whites dominated the conference; of the twenty-four published speeches, only five were by blacks. Monroe Trotter was concerned that whites were founding and managing an organization to do what, he believed, blacks could and should be doing for themselves. White dominance in the meeting prompted a black woman (believed to be Ida Wells Barnett) to shout, "They are betraying us again—these white friends of ours."[50]

DuBois viewed the situation differently. Based on his experiences with the Niagara Movement and the success of Booker T. Washington, DuBois recognized the need for financial stability. Unless there was money to support an organization, it was not likely to succeed no matter how lofty its ideas and goals might be. At last, liberal whites were offering their financial assistance to blacks who spoke contrary to Booker T. Washington.

DuBois expressed his enthusiasm in a *Horizon* article: "The vision . . . a new alliance between experienced social workers and reformers in touch on the one hand with scientific philanthropy and on the other hand with the great struggling mass of laborers of all kinds, whose conditions and needs know no color line."

Besides, DuBois had had a rapport with white liberals for many years. When very few journals would publish DuBois's work, William Ward, editor of *The Independent* regularly featured his writings. Mary Ovington had spoken at Atlanta University and it is believed she was a paid member of the Niagara Movement and a subscriber to the *Horizon*.

So, for the time being, DuBois was willing to sacrifice total control for a well-financed organization through which progress could be made, and he felt that eventually control of the organization could be shifted. His colleagues, Ida Wells Barnett and Monroe Trotter, refused to give an inch. They wanted black control of any organization formed to benefit the black community.

At a second conference held in May 1910, the National Association for the Advancement of Colored People (the NAACP) was formed. Moorfield Storey, a Boston lawyer, was elected president and permanent offices were opened at number 20 Vesey Street in New York City. DuBois was the only black officer and incorporator. Many of the Niagara Movement members joined the NAACP on the strength of DuBois's involvement, but others, like Monroe Trotter refused to join, for he never trusted white leadership.

From the start, the NAACP was "a single articulate group of those Americans, white and black, whose democratic faith abhorred the color line." Its purpose was to "remove hindrances to the free development of the individual—discrimination, especially segregation." No special privileges were asked for, just justice and equality for all Americans regardless of race, creed or national origin.

To this end, the NAACP proposed to use legal action, education, and appeals to state and federal legislatures to remove unjust laws. And, finally, it was believed that by informing the American people about the abuses of African-American rights, there would be a general cry from the populace to make changes.

At first, DuBois was offered the position of Association Secretary, but he declined, saying he wanted to write and speak. He encouraged the board to invest in a journal much like the *Horizon*. Some members of the board of directors were concerned that DuBois might use the monthly journal in his ongoing attack on Washington. His promise that he would "avoid personal rancor of all sorts" helped the board make the decision. It was agreed that *The Crisis Magazine: A Record of the Darker Race* would become the publishing arm of the NAACP, and that DuBois would be its editor.[51]

According to biographer Broderick, *The Crisis* gave DuBois a "secure editorial chair and an independent forum." Of his new position DuBois wrote: "With this monthly magazine, I could discuss the Negro problem and tell white people and colored people just what the NAACP was and what it proposed to do." The *Horizon* folded in July 1910, and *Crisis* made the perfect transition.

Although it meant leaving Atlanta University and his research work, DuBois felt it was time for a change. And, he was particularly ready for the new challenges that awaited him in New York City.

# eight

## AFRICA'S SON

Until quite recently, African-American children were taught to be ashamed of their ethnic and cultural roots. (In fact, it wasn't until the 1960s that Negroid features—broad noses, high cheekbones, dark skin, kinky hair, and full lips—were considered beautiful.)

Africa was stereotyped as a primitive place, and the people were characterized as wild savages having made no significant contribution to world civilization. Many of these misconceptions got into books and films. Misinformation led people to arrive at erroneous assumptions. For example: Africa is a continent and not a country; tigers are Asiatic and not African animals; Egyptians are Africans the same as Italians are Europeans; and the continent is not predominantly jungle.

As always, DuBois was a generation ahead of his peers in acknowledging Africa as his homeland. In 1900 he wrote:

The spell of Africa is upon me. The ancient witchery of her medicine is burning my drowsy, dreamy blood. This is not a country, it is a world—a universe of itself and for itself,

it is Different, Immense, Menacing, Allur-
ing. It is a great black bosom where the spirit
longs to die. It is a life so burning, so fire
encircled that one bursts with terrible soul
inflaming life. One longs to leap against the
sun, and then calls, like some great hand of
fate, the slow, silent, crushing power of al-
mighty sleep—of silence, of immoveable
Power beyond, within, around. Then comes
the calm. The dreamless beat of midday still-
ness, at dusk, at dawn, at noon, always . . .
Africa is the Spiritual Frontier of human
kind.

When U.S. Senator James K. Vardaman said in 1914
before Congress, "The Negro . . . never had any
civilization except that which had been inculcated
by a superior race . . ." DuBois responded by writing
*The Negro* (1915), telling the story of three great
West African nations: Ghana, Mali, and Songhay.
*The Negro* was a commendable work because it presented a positive picture of the "dark continent,"
and introduced readers to the glorious civilizations
of sub-Saharan Africa that flourished during the
European Dark Ages.

DuBois believed it was in black America's best
interest to support African nationalism. Once free
of European dominance, emerging African nations
could provide markets for black American-made
products, goods and services.

DuBois felt that it was economically feasible, and
he also believed that it was psychologically healthy
for blacks to be culturally and spiritually linked to
their ancestral home. That is the reason he became
very active in the formation of Pan-Africanism, the

general purpose of which was to unify people of color against imperialism all over the world.

The first meeting of the Pan-African Movement was held in England in 1900. W.E.B. DuBois's involvement in the world struggle for equality and human rights would remain a driving force throughout his life.

DuBois had become interested in imperialism while a student in Berlin. He was opposed to it then but there was no vehicle through which he could channel his opposition. He again went to Europe in 1900, this time with Harold Williams, a West Indian lawyer, with the hope of gathering support for African independence. The group petitioned Queen Victoria, but with little result.

"We protested," DuBois wrote in the summary of the meeting, "the treatment of the natives in the organization of South Africa, but we lost out on our hopes of a permanent organization."

Those first delegates called for the darker races to organize as a means to effectively fight imperialism in Asia as well as Africa. In DuBois's address before the 1900 meeting he stated, "The problem of the Twentieth Century is the problem of the color line."[53]

Meanwhile, between the years 1910 and 1919, DuBois remained the editor of *The Crisis* magazine. His numerous editorials and articles reflect DuBois's and the NAACP's position on African and Asian colonialism, European imperialism and such domestic issues as voting rights, women's rights, lynchings and rioting, and the death of Booker T. Washington in 1915. DuBois supported women's suffrage and frequently highlighted the work of Mary Church Terrell, president of the National Association of

Colored Women's Clubs, Ida Wells Barnett, who was chairperson of the resolutions committee, and Jane Addams, a social worker.

DuBois was happy to see black voters finally abandoning their blind loyalty to the Republican Party of Abraham Lincoln. Since his college years, DuBois had been calling for blacks to align themselves with those political candidates who supported them in their struggle for freedom and justice within the American democracy.

Woodrow Wilson, a Democrat, won the presidency in 1912. Black support turned to black disillusionment when under Wilson's administration, Washington, D.C., the seat of democracy, became a segregated city.

DuBois warned in a *Crisis* editorial that "racial intolerance will lead to unprecedented violence" if something wasn't done to stop the activities of racist organizations bent on "annihilating the entire colored race." His predictions were all too real to those who daily were confronted with hate and violence from organizations such as the Ku Klux Klan.

The Ku Klux Klan had reorganized in 1915 at a meeting on Stone Mountain, Georgia, and the terrorist organization grew stronger than it had been in the 1870s. By 1920, lynchings in the South were as commonplace as picnics.

Between 1917 and 1919 the United States was involved in World War I. A. Philip Randolph, a black

*Early issue of the* Crisis *magazine, organ of the NAACP. DuBois was its editor.*

# THE CRISIS

## A RECORD OF THE DARKER RACES

Volume One     NOVEMBER, 1910   543626   Number One

Edited by W. E. BURGHARDT DU BOIS, with the co-operation of Oswald Garrison Villard, J. Max Barber, Charles Edward Russell, Kelly Miller, W. S. Braithwaite and M. D. Maclean.

## CONTENTS

PUBLISHED MONTHLY BY THE

## National Association for the Advancement of Colored People

AT TWENTY VESEY STREET           NEW YORK CITY

ONE DOLLAR A YEAR          TEN CENTS A COPY

*Editorial offices of the
Crisis in New York City.
DuBois is standing at the right.*

labor advocate and editor of the *Messenger,* told young black men to refuse service in a segregated army. He was labeled a radical and called "dangerous." DuBois pointed out the absurdity of black soldiers fighting in segregated units and returning home to hostility and anger. But he stopped short of telling blacks not to defend their country. In fact, he encouraged black men and women to serve the nation with pride and dignity during this period of crisis.

Racial intolerance against blacks reached a feverish level in 1919 when there were at least twenty-five race riots all over the country. It was during this climate of terror that the NAACP sent DuBois to Europe to collect materials for a history of the Negro in war. They also authorized DuBois to call for a second Pan-African Congress to be held in 1921.

Since DuBois had taken the job as editor of the *Crisis,* he'd used it as a "valuable source of Pan-African ideas." With the aid of Blaise Diagne, a member of the French Parliament from Senegal, he arranged the Conference in Paris. Fifty-seven delegates were present, including sixteen black Americans, twenty West Indians and twelve Africans. The congress passed a resolution that allowed Africans to participate in their own government "as fast as their development permits." They called for a law to prevent the "exploitation of foreign capital," one "to end slavery and capital punishment" and another to grant "the right to an education."

DuBois came home feeling satisfied with their efforts. And so was the NAACP, for that same year, he was awarded the Spingarn Medal, the highest honor given by the organization, for his work in establishing the Congress.

Then came the emergence of the "Back to Africa Movement" led by Marcus Garvey. Garvey came to Harlem from Jamaica in 1916. In 1921, he called an international convention to form The Black Star Line steamship company for the purpose of transporting American blacks to Africa, who it was hoped, with the help of native Africans, would take control of the continent from the colonial powers.

Garvey was a flamboyant man who won the admiration and respect of poor inner-city blacks. Stories about "the Return" gave hopeless people something to dream about.[54]

His wasn't the first of the back-to-Africa movements in America, nor was he the first to introduce the notion that being black was beautiful or that being of African descent was a source of pride. But few leaders inspired the love and trust of the masses the way Garvey could.

Most back-to-Africa attempts had failed for the most part. But there was the success story of Liberia, which had been settled by former American slaves who'd chosen to return to Africa. The capital city, Monrovia, was named after United States President James Monroe, who was in office during the formation of Liberia, and who had fully supported the movement. Liberia was the exception and not the rule.

While it was generally agreed that the United States needed to change, abandoning it was not an

*A 1936 photo of Marcus Garvey,*
*Leader of the Back to Africa movement.*
*His slogan was "Do for Self."*

alternative considered by many African-Americans until Garvey came along.

Membership in his Universal Negro Improvement association (UNIA) numbered in the millions, and within a few short years, branch offices had sprung up all over the nation. The UNI emphasis was on black economic growth and development, self-pride and cultural awareness. Garvey encouraged people to develop businesses and light industry so they would be ready to help their African brothers build industries and factories once they arrived. Money poured in and his followers participated readily in his many business ventures.

The black *intelligentsia* scoffed at Garvey and called him a charlatan and a thief. Monroe Trotter was very outspoken about Garvey's agenda. For a while DuBois took a "wait and see" position, and even-handedly evaluated Garvey's programs, pointing out the strengths and weaknesses as he interpreted them. He liked, for example, many of Garvey's self-help programs.

Garvey encouraged his followers "to clean up, fix up, and stop begging white people to help them! DO FOR SELF!" The results were enough to make believers out of his most severe critics. Though segregation was objectionable to DuBois and contrary to NAACP philosophy, he had to admit that under Garvey's racial isolation practices a great deal had been accomplished in Harlem and other ghetto areas.

Yet, as time progressed and no emigration to Africa had begun, Garvey's critics increased. In the end, DuBois totally rejected Garvey and his movement, calling him "spiritually bankrupt" and his program "futile."

In spite of the attacks, Garvey remained popular, but later he was imprisoned for using the United States mails to defraud. He served two years in prison and then was deported. Marcus Garvey lived in London until 1940 when he died, poor and alone.[55]

Pan-Africanism and the Garvey plan were vastly different, still some people managed to confuse the two or to think of them as the same. Unlike Garvey, DuBois didn't advocate the exodus of blacks from America. He sought, instead, a cooperative effort among people of color in the struggle against imperialism wherever it was found on the globe.

The NAACP board didn't seem to be clear on this issue so it cooled toward DuBois's Pan-African involvement, fearing the association with Garvey's brand of radicalism would cost the organization much needed financial support.

DuBois was furious with the board. He refused to terminate his international activities regarding Africa, and continued using the *Crisis* to support African independence.

James Weldon Johnson, who had joined the NAACP in 1916, was named the first black NAACP Executive Director on November 6, 1920. Johnson helped relieve some of the tension between black membership (represented by DuBois) and the white-dominated board of directors. Johnson, a graduate of Atlanta University, knew Dr. DuBois well; they respected each other and shared many ideas, especially their love of writing. Johnson was the author of the popular book *The Autobiography of an ex-Colored Man*, a fictional look at black American life at the turn of the century.

Still Johnson could not influence DuBois to curb

his Pan-African involvement. According to biographer Broderick, "[DuBois] likened Pan-Africanism to Zionism, 'the centralization of race effort and the recognition of a racial fount'."

The NAACP disassociated itself from the Pan-African Movement, but DuBois, at his own expense, attended the 1923 conference held in Lisbon, Portugal. This time, three Americans made up the executive committee and only thirteen countries participated.

There was a fourth meeting held in New York City in 1927 to settle "the question as to whether Negroes are to lead in the rise of Africa or whether they must always and everywhere follow the guidance of white folk." A fifth conference was planned but not held. Some observers suggest that infighting, petty jealousies, power struggles, and a general lack of direction weakened the group, but Will DuBois felt there were other reasons why Pan-Africanism wasn't widely supported. And he wasn't shy about giving those reasons in *The Crisis*. He blamed governmental opposition, lack of philanthropy, and "a deliberate boycott of white men determined to act for Africa without consulting black men, and the lack of understanding by educated and thinking Negroes."

He also believed Garvey's movement "muddied the waters . . . beyond recovery." But that didn't mean DuBois had given up on his commitment to African independence. And he continued using the *Crisis* to support this pet cause. His tenacity only served to increase the growing rife between DuBois and the NAACP board.

Watchers of the NAACP noted at the time that the course black advancement should take, and control of the *Crisis* were the two issues in desperate need of resolution or many felt, the organization could not advance the cause of anybody. DuBois would make no compromises, especially about control of the *Crisis*.

Under his editorship and management, the magazine was self-supporting and required no funds from the organization; even DuBois's salary came from *Crisis* income. He argued, then, that while the NAACP owned the magazine, he was responsible for its content. His reasoning was that as he had been financially responsible for the success or failure of the publication, the Association never having financially contributed a cent, it was, therefore, morally right that the "legal ownership rightly followed such financial risk." DuBois never went so far as to suggest that he actually owned *The Crisis*, but he used this argument to keep editorial control.

The 1920s was one of the busiest periods in DuBois's life. He spent a lot of time away from Nina and Yolande. But when he was at home, he knew how to enjoy himself, especially at a time when African-American poets, artists, dancers, photographers, musicians, and singers were experiencing a "Renaissance."

# nine

## THE RENAISSANCE

The 1920s have been designated the "Renaissance" of African-American culture. It was a terrible time to live in Dixie, but it was a great time to live in The Big Apple (New York City), especially if you were young, talented and black. Poor sharecroppers left the South—many of them fleeing a few steps ahead of the Klan. Whole families ran for their lives in the night, sometimes leaving everything behind—even supper on the table—so as not to rouse suspicion. Some parents sent their children to relatives "up North," hoping they might have a better chance for education and employment. By 1923 Harlem was bustling, teeming with life and talent.

The Cotton Club was the place to go. Whites—including European royalty—poured into the Harlem nightclub to catch the acts of Earl Hines, Count Basie and his orchestra, or the high-kicking chorus line. Maybe a night out meant going to hear a young trumpeter named Louis "Satchmo" Armstrong down at Connie's Inn, or see him perform "Ain't Misbehavin'" in the hit musical *Hot Chocolate*.

DuBois and James Weldon Johnson had been two of the most significant writers between 1900 and 1922, but with the publication of *Harlem Shadows*,

Claude McKay made his literary debut. His "If We Must Die" became a battle cry for those who stood against oppression.

### If We Must Die

*If we must die, let it not be like hogs*
*Hunted and penned in an inglorious spot,*
*While round us bark the mad and hungry dogs,*
*Making their mock at our accursed lot.*
*If we must die—O let us nobly die.*
*So that our precious blood may not be shed*
*In vain; then even the monsters we defy*
*Shall be constrained to honor us though dead!*
*Oh, Kinsmen! We must meet the common foe;*
*Though far outnumbered let us show us brave.*
*And for their thousand blows deal one death-blow!*
*What though before us lies the open grave?*
*Like men we'll face the murderous, cowardly pack,*
*Pressed to the wall, dying, but fighting back!*

McKay captured the fighting spirit of the 1920s. Booker T. Washington's counsel was rejected by people tired of waiting for what they had fought and died for: liberty, justice and freedom. Young black men and women would not accept apologies for segregation.

Following McKay came other poets and novelists such as Jean Toomer and Countee Cullen, but the most remembered "Renaissance" poet would be Langston Hughes. Hughes used the language masterfully, zinging his point across the plate with powerful words used sparingly.

Before his death in 1967, Langston Hughes wrote a story of NAACP and also dedicate his poem, "The Negro Speaks of Rivers" to Dr. DuBois.

*I've known rivers:*
*I've known rivers ancient as the world and older*
*than the flow of human blood in human veins.*

*My soul has grown deep like the rivers.*

*I bathed in the Euphrates when dawns were young.*
*I built my hut near the Congo and it lulled me to*
*sleep.*
*I looked upon the Nile and raised the pyramids*
*above it.*
*I heard the singing of the Mississippi when Abe*
*Lincoln went down to New Orleans, and I've*
*seen its muddy bosom turn all golden in the*
*sunset.*

*I've known rivers:*
*Ancient, dusky rivers.*

*My soul has grown deep like the rivers.*

Nothing satisfied Dr. DuBois more than to be right in the middle of the Harlem Renaissance. Being in the company of such bright and talented people, filled with hope and promise, overjoyed him. DuBois had missed teaching young, eager minds and most of the time he felt drained from fighting archaic ideas that should have been laid to rest decades ago. How refreshing it was to be around the sounds and colors of a new era. These young poets were favored by DuBois and he featured their poetry and reviewed their works regularly in *The Crisis*.

DuBois was pleased that his daughter, Yolande was part of the "New Negro" intellectual movement. She, like her peers, was well-educated and well-spoken. She graduated from Fisk University in 1926 and was teaching in New York City. DuBois adored his daughter, and readily admitted that she was lovingly spoiled. To show how spoiled she really was he liked to tell this story:

> . . .we stopped a while to breathe the salt air at Atlantic City. This tot of four years marched beside me down the Boardwalk amid the unmoved and almost unnoticing crowd. She was puzzled. Never before in her memory had the world treated her quite so differently. [She was not noticed by anyone.] "Papa," she exclaimed at last impatiently, "I guess they don't know I'm here."[56]

The extravagant wedding of Yolande and Countee Cullen in 1928 was a lavish display of fatherly indulgence. At age twenty-five, Countee Cullen was one of the leading "Renaissance" poets and also one of the most eligible bachelors in town. After graduating from New York University with honors, he had received his master's degree from Harvard in 1926.

DuBois suggested that Yolande and Countee have a small wedding, but Yolande had other ideas. Her wedding party included sixteen bridesmaids. Three thousand saw the marriage and a thousand people waited on the street outside Salem Baptist Church, where Countee's father, Rev. Frederick A. Cullen, performed the ceremony.

DuBois described the revelry:

> There were poets and teachers, actors, art-
> ists, and students.
>     But it was not simply conventional Amer-
> ica—it had a dark and shimmering beauty all
> its own; a calm and high restraint and sense
> of new power; it was a new race; a new
> thought; a new thing rejoicing in a ceremony
> as old as the world. (And after it all and before
> it, such a jolly, happy crowd; some of the girls
> even smoked cigarettes!)[57]

There was some criticism of the four-page spread
devoted to an article and photos of Yolande's wedding in the *Crisis*. Some NAACP chapters felt there
was more pressing information concerning the race
for which the space could have been used.

Accepting criticism was a virtue DuBois never
mastered. He responded arrogantly and with a stub-
born defiance of authority. "The *Crisis*," he wrote,
"was for sophisticated people and not for fools." His
attitude didn't earn him friends when he most
needed them.

The frivolity of the Roaring Twenties gave way
to crushing despair after the 1929 stock market
crash. America was hurled into a financial abyss—
The Great Depression. The loss of jobs took its toll
on all segments of the population, but what jobs that
were available were not given to blacks.

Few families had extra money to support organizations, so NAACP membership declined. Fewer
still could afford magazine subscriptions. The *Crisis*
had fewer than 21,000 subscribers by 1932. As long

as the *Crisis* had been self-supporting, DuBois had a free rein, independent of NAACP control. Now he needed money to keep the journal going, so he called for help. He got the money he needed, but it was personally very costly.

# ten

## BACK TO ATLANTA

In 1934, the NAACP board ruled that all *Crisis* editorials had to be read and approved by the board before publication. DuBois was warned against using the journal to strike at his opponents; in-house business was to be kept private, and personality differences were not to be aired in public. Dr. DuBois reluctantly agreed to all the restrictions just to keep the *Crisis* going. It was a blow to his pride.

It was about this time that Dr. DuBois's racial tone began to shift. In 1930 he was sixty-two years old. For over four decades, every attempt to work for a peaceful, truly united America had met with overwhelming resistance. Each step forward had resulted in what seemed two steps backward. His writings during the early thirties showed that he was moving away from the idealism of his youth. Blacks and whites working together, cooperating to better mankind had not brought about the changes he'd once hoped for. The belief that education made a person less likely to be prejudiced proved to be untrue.

In 1933 he wrote: "Segregation without discrimination—voluntary segregation—should not evoke opposition." He had come to believe that the path to black advancement was within the race itself. "There seems no hope that America in our day will yield in its color or race hatred any substantial ground and we have no physical nor economic classes that will force compliance with decent civilized ideals in church, state, industry or art."[58]

Shocking though it may have seemed at the time, DuBois was sounding much like the separatists he had for years opposed. *Crisis* articles began to reflect his new philosophy of racial separateness— he called for all-black unions to form and business ventures that catered specifically to African-American needs. Economic independence and racial self-reliance seemed the only alternatives left to a people who had begged for equality and who had been ignored for years.

His new position was contrary to the NAACP directive which called for blacks and whites working together to end segregation. Thus it wasn't surprising to anyone when the board responded. They insisted that a disclaimer be run in the *Crisis*, and a series of articles clearly stating "The NAACP . . . is squarely opposed to segregation—voluntary or otherwise."

Then, to add insult to injury, a four-member committee was formed to manage *The Crisis*. DuBois then went public with his objections, hoping to rally support. His hostile relationship with the board was glossed over but differences were mounting, especially after James Weldon Johnson resigned in 1933. Walter White took his place and the conflict heightened.

Walter White was born in 1893 in Atlanta, Georgia. White joined the NAACP as a special investigator of lynchings in Arkansas. Members of the

NAACP were despised by many southern whites. That's why southern NAACP members secretly paid their dues and hid their identity as subscribers to *The Crisis*. Once members were discovered, they were harassed and sometimes even lost their jobs. In White's case, once it was found out that he was a NAACP employee he barely escaped being lynched himself.[59]

Walter White was fiery, strong-willed, and in matters of racial equality his motto was "Now is the time!" In 1932, White said DuBois was the "chief molder of modern thought regarding the Negro." It would seem that White and DuBois would have been excellent working companions, but that was not the case. The conflict between the two men mounted daily; DuBois turning more toward black separatism, and White holding firmly to the NAACP charter as his guideline.

Rev. Francis J. Grimke, one of the founders of the NAACP, and a good friend, said to DuBois that if he tried to lead blacks back to segregation it would be the end to his leadership, because they had "followed too long the old DuBois's uncompromising fight for full equality to turn to a new DuBois who sounded like Booker T. Washington."

But some of DuBois's supporters thought he was right. R.J. Simmons, president of the Duluth, Minnesota, branch of the NAACP wrote him, saying, "We have followed with interest, the various discussions on segregation, and have tried, along with the rest to arrive at a safe interpretation of proper attitudes and procedure. Certainly, it is a difficult proposition to solve, and, from our viewpoint, will be for many years. But at present we believe you have hit upon the sanest and most practical course for a peaceable and permanent solution of our case, viz, work out our salvation behind the barriers of prejudice which all the efforts of previous years have failed to break down."[60]

In July 1934, at the age of sixty-six, W.E.B. resigned from the NAACP. His resignation was met with mixed feelings. Carrie W. Clifford, a good friend and fellow NAACP founder summarized how many people felt about his leaving. "Poor race, what now?" The Chicago *Defender* ran a cartoon showing the picture of Booker T. Washington over which was the question, "Was he right after all?" Over a picture of DuBois was the question, "Is he a quitter?"

Some NAACP leaders were glad to see DuBois leave. Even his good friend, Mary Ovington, a founding member, wrote to another founder, "Now that we are rid of our octopus, for of late he [DuBois] has been draining our strength, I hope we shall do better work."[61]

The old warrior was battle weary and longed for a time when he could just *be*. In fact, he built a house in Baltimore, Maryland, for himself and Nina. Countee Cullen had died. Yolande had remarried, was a mother, and was teaching nearby. Within the year DuBois accepted a position at Atlanta University as head of the sociology department. His good friend, John Hope, was then the president.

DuBois returned to Atlanta alone. Nina remained in Baltimore near Yolande. During the next ten years DuBois wrote two more books, the most significant being *Black Reconstruction* (1935). He won awards by the score, wrote a weekly newspaper column, lectured, took a world tour, and founded yet another journal—*The Pylon*, a review of race and culture. Biographer Broderick summarized DuBois's work during the decade between 1934 and 1944 as a diffusion of his talents ". . . the classroom teacher trained a new generation of leadership, the historian built up the race's past and investigated its present, the journalist picked his way through the swift changes of the New Deal and puzzled over the worldwide significance of the color line as the second World War approached."

And when the United States entered World War II, DuBois called for blacks to "close ranks," and "fight for democracy not only for white folks but for yellow, brown, and black."

In August 1944, Atlanta University asked DuBois to resign. Speculations still abound but the real reason for the resignation has never been made public. Some DuBois biographers believe his criticism of Atlanta University's educational system might have been the cause. Once again, Dr. DuBois considered retirement. But another old friend, Arthur Spingarn, invited him to return to the NAACP as the director of research, "free to write and speak as he wished and to devote himself to special foreign aspects of the race problem." DuBois, who was then close to seventy-six years of age, accepted the position.

In August 1944, he was quoted in the Harlem Amsterdam: "The greatest question before the world is whether democracy in Europe and America can survive as long as the majority of the people of the world are kept in colonial status. This is the problem to which I propose to devote the remaining years of my active life." And he did.

# eleven

## DISILLUSIONMENT

DuBois returned to a different NAACP. Many of the faces were unfamiliar. Some, he was happy to see, were his former students. His beloved *Crisis* was in the capable hands of Roy Wilkins, who in 1955 would follow White as Executive Director of the NAACP. DuBois put the past behind him and leaped into his new responsibilities with the vigor of a man half his age.

While so many things were new to him, the old conflict between White and DuBois didn't take long to surface. As White asserted his leadership, DuBois resisted, refusing to "go along just to get along." DuBois's first assignment was to direct work on a "Committee to Present the Cause of the Negro at the Next Peace Conference." In this capacity he represented the NAACP and sought out other organizations with the same goals.

Following World War II, a nervous peace existed between the superpowers: England, France, Russia, and the United States. But, the Nazi atrocities, combined with the threat of nuclear annihilation, forced the world's leaders to consider peaceful alternatives to future conflicts. Peace was in season.

In the spring of 1945, the founding conference

of the United Nations was held in San Francisco, California. The idea of an international organization whose purpose would be to help nations seek peaceful solutions to their problems was the brainchild of U.S. President Franklin D. Roosevelt. Unfortunately he had died on April 12, 1945. As a tribute to her husband, Eleanor Roosevelt insisted that the conference continue on schedule. On April 25, 1945, the former First Lady led the United States delegation.

Several African-American delegates were included as consultants. Among them were W.E.B. DuBois and Walter White of the NAACP; well-known educator and presidential advisor Mary McLeod Bethune, and diplomat and future winner of the Nobel Peace Prize, Ralph Bunche.

Although the conflict between Walter White and Dr. DuBois was serious, they managed to present a united front at the conference, especially in their position against colonialization. In 1945 most African and Asian countries were still under European domination.

The African-American delegates submitted a statute which they hoped would be adopted into the United Nations charter. The statement forbade any nation from denying the people of another nation the right of representation in their government. In 1776, the thirteen American colonies had demanded the same rights from England. Nevertheless, the proposal was rejected.

DuBois appealed to John Foster Dulles and other United States delegates for support. He wrote: "The attempt to write an International Bill of Rights into the San Francisco conference without any specific mention of the people living in colonies seems to me a most unfortunate procedure. If it were clearly understood that freedom of speech, freedom from want and freedom from fear, which the nations are asked to guarantee, would without question be extended to the 750 million people who live in colonial areas, this would be a great and fateful step."

The appeal was not heeded, and the United Nations Charter was approved without giving the organization the power to intervene to protect citizens of colonized nations. Colonies were considered "internal" or "domestic" in nature and not subject to international intervention.

DuBois returned to New York angry and disappointed. He had come to believe that good sense and sound judgment were not always the choices of governments. Hadn't history shown time and time again that oppression bred revolution? That is what had happened in Russia, he frequently pointed out.

Later in the same year, his spirits were lifted when in October he was invited to be the keynote speaker at the Fifth Pan-African Congress, this time held in Manchester, England. There he got to meet with some of Africa's emerging black leaders, Kenyatta of Kenya, Johnson of Liberia, and Nkrumah of Ghana. The highest honor came when he was elected president of the organization.

Back at home, the conflict in the NAACP offices continued between DuBois and White, this time over the activities of the controversial entertainer and political activist Paul Robeson.

Paul Robeson was a gifted musician, internationally recognized as one of the best concert baritones of his day. He was also an outspoken activist who used his celebrity status to attack racism and discrimination wherever it existed. Robeson invited

*Paul Robeson (1898–1976),
athlete, singer, actor, and
political activist.*

his friend Dr. DuBois to join in an antilynching demonstration at Madison Square Garden and another in Washington, D.C. on September 23, 1946. DuBois agreed to participate in the demonstrations, not knowing that Walter White had, in the name of the NAACP, formed the National Emergency Committee Against Mob Violence.

When White heard about the Robeson-sponsored protests, he sent DuBois a memo on September 19, 1946, stating: "On August 6, the NAACP invited some fifty or more organizations to send representatives to a meeting held here to discuss joint action against the rising tide of mob violence. It was said by a number of those present that it was one of the most broadly representative groups that had ever been gathered. Out of that meeting came the National Emergency Committee Against Mob Violence. . ."

White went on to explain the NAACP's position regarding lynching. He ended with a slight reprimand. "It would be most helpful on issues which are an integral part of the Association's work . . . if inquiry could be made by you on such matters inasmuch as the calling of this conference has tremendously complicated and overburdened the office. It would just save us time and headaches if the facts are obtained before a decision is made."

DuBois was livid. He was doing what his title and job description said he was to do. Three days later, he fired a tart memo back to White, saying: "Your memorandum of September 19 was the first notice I have had of your new antilynching movement. My cooperation was evidently not needed. It was certainly not asked. If I had been notified, I would gladly have cooperated. On the other hand, I have been fighting lynching for forty years, and I have a right to let the world know that I am still fighting. I therefore gladly endorsed the Robeson movement, which asked for my cooperation. This did not and could not have interfered with the NAACP program. The fight against mob law is the monopoly of no one person—no one organization."[61]

There was more behind the conflict than is evident in these letters. White felt that he had a legitimate concern, because to the general public, DuBois and the NAACP were synonymous, due to his long association with the organization. When Dr. DuBois spoke, acted, or wrote anything, it was automatically considered the position of the NAACP as well. White especially wanted to maintain a clear distinction between Robeson's organization known as the Crusade Against Lynching, and the NAACP's committee. But especially so after the September 1947 meeting with President Truman and Robeson and the headlines that followed.

As had been planned, Robeson and several other representatives from black organizations (the NAACP excluded) met with President Harry Truman. They asked him to take a public stand against lynching. It was later reported that Truman appeared cool to the idea, and Robeson took exception to the president's attitude and heatedly responded that blacks couldn't be expected to defend a country that didn't defend them. Truman shook his fist at Robeson and dismissed the meeting angrily.

Reporters seized the opportunity to ask Robeson a question which was being asked more and more often of him. "Are you a communist?" Robeson repeatedly said he was not a member of the Communist Party, but he publicly supported the Soviet government, saying, "In Russia, full employment is a fact, and not a myth, and discrimination is non-existent."[62]

By midcentury, the mood toward the Soviet Union had changed from when they had been allies during World War II. Then, the United States had been the only country with atomic weapons. Using spies, the Soviet Union stole the secrets of how to make atomic weapons and other military classified information. Would the Soviets use their military might to overthrow democracy and impose communism on the people of America? Fear formed a wall between the two countries called the "iron curtain" by Prime Minister Winston Churchill.

The Socialist Party had existed in the United States since the late 1800s. During the 1920s there had been a strong socialist push, but it never really offered a threat to the existing government. For example, labor leader Eugene Debs had run for president on the Socialist ticket many times, but had never garnered many votes.

The Communist Party of the United States also existed openly and freely. Communism was not considered a direct threat until after the war. By 1948 the fear of communism was growing. Tolerance of socialism in any form was considered un-American.

Paul Robeson was not a man to scare easily or to back down from his beliefs. When asked if he was a member of the Communist Party, he answered that he was not. He was warned to stop praising the Soviet government and to stop attacking the United States government. But he simply pointed to the facts. "Right now," he said, "the Communist Party is against lynching. I'm against lynching." At the time, lynchings were still taking place all over the United States on a regular basis and still nothing was being done about it. While some people admired Robeson and cheered his bold confrontations with government officials, others labeled him a trouble-maker and set out to destroy him.

W.E.B. DuBois was a sincere admirer of Paul Robeson. They each shared the same fierce opposition to racial discrimination, injustice, and colonialism and each was willing to put at risk their personal safety and to sacrifice their career security to fight for peace and justice. They also shared a warm relationship with the Russian people. During their independent travels in the Soviet Union, DuBois and Robeson were accepted as equals. This was at a time in United States history when black men and women were horribly abused and were treated as inferiors.

DuBois had been fascinated by socialism and the Russian revolution for many years. He'd embraced the concept of socialism as early as 1905, and had, in 1911, briefly joined New York Local No. 1 of the Socialist Party. He defined socialism in broad terms as "the assertion by the community of its right to control business and industry; the denial of the old assumption that public business can ever be a private enterprise."

After returning from his 1926 visit to the Soviet Union, Dr. DuBois wrote, ". . . if Bolshevik means people striving with partial success to organize industry for public service rather than for private profit . . . then I am a Bolshevik." And for years DuBois was an advocate of the socialist labor movement in America.

At the 1949 Congress of the
Partisans of Peace in Paris,
Paul Robeson (center) introduces
DuBois (right), the American
delegate, to Peter Blackman,
British West Indies delegate.

At about the same time DuBois began to favor black separatism, he also began questioning whether African-Americans should trust *any* political system dominated by whites.

DuBois was at all times a scholar—a sociologist—who used his intellect to scrutinize the political systems of his day and to objectively report how each might help end discrimination in America and around the world. He compared communism, capitalism, democracy and cited the benefits each held for black Americans.

For example, he pointed to white labor—led by American socialists—which still discriminated against black workers. Following a stinging article in which he warned blacks to be careful about joining "people's movements," he was barraged with criticism.

One Communist writer accused him of being a "betrayer of the Negro people," because he spoke out against a Socialist third party. DuBois reasoned that a third party presidential ticket didn't have a chance to win and would only split the Northern vote and ensure the continued election of Southern-backed Democrats. So he didn't support the idea.

But it was inconceivable to him to stop associating with people he respected because they belonged to a political party out of favor with the American government. It is unfortunate that his position caused him so much trouble.

Continued conflicts resulted in DuBois's resignation from the NAACP in September 1948. He was given a pension and sent on his way. Again, there was no chance to consider retirement because Robeson immediately invited him to be the director of the Council on African Affairs. Without a moment's hesitation, Dr. DuBois accepted. He had been working voluntarily for the organization anyway.

The Council on African Affairs had been founded in 1939 by Robeson, Max Yergan of the black YMCA, Alphaeus Hunton of Howard University, and financially supported by Frederick V. Field, founder of Marshall-Field Department Stores. The purpose of the organization was three-fold: to aid African colonies in their fight for independence, to encourage better understanding of African cultures among American blacks, and to protest American segregation and lynching.

DuBois moved his office and began work within the week. He loved working for the Council, mainly because he was given the freedom to write without restrictions. Meanwhile, in 1949, DuBois attended a Peace Conference in Paris, and then went on to visit Moscow where he was greeted and treated like visiting royalty. Robeson, who was also touring Europe, spoke briefly at the conference, saying, "It is unthinkable that American Negroes will go to war on behalf of those who have oppressed us for generations . . . against a country (the Soviet Union) which in one generation has raised our people to full human dignity of mankind." His words were twisted to mean that no black man would fight for America against Russia. The American press painted Robeson as a traitor.

Walter White at the NAACP denounced Robeson's statement and argued that African-Americans would meet their responsibilities in wartime like any other citizens. Black journalists also attacked Robeson, who denied he spoke for anyone other than himself. Even those who had admired Robeson and agreed with him on such issues as lynching and discrimination, were coerced to renounce his statement before the House Un-American Activities Committee.

Finally there was a mob reaction in August 1949 to a Robeson concert in Peekskill, New York. The Ku Klux Klan burned a cross and called Robeson a traitor. There was a riot which resulted in physical attacks and stonings.[63]

Dr. DuBois used the power of his pen to attack those who accused Robeson of disloyalty. "The real disloyalty to the nation," he wrote, "were the lawless cross-burners who terrorized innocent people" while law enforcement officers looked the other way.

# twelve

## THE TRIAL

Nina DuBois had a stroke in the winter of 1948–9. DuBois brought her to New York to be treated, and canceled all his engagements to be with his ailing wife. Soon Nina grew lonely and longed to again be near Yolande, who was still teaching in Baltimore. As soon as she was able to travel, DuBois accompanied Nina to their home in Morgan Park, Baltimore. Nina died in the spring of 1949 and DuBois was described as "inconsolable." Theirs had not been a perfect marriage, but it had been a good one. She was buried in the family plot in Great Barrington next to their son.

Meanwhile the Peace Information Center was being established in New York by American delegates who had attended the Paris Peace Conference. The purpose of the center was "to bring information to the people concerning worldwide efforts to prevent further wars." Dr. DuBois agreed to become the chairman of the center. And at age eighty-two he agreed to run for the United States Senate on the Labor Party ticket in August 1950. He received 205,729 votes. "It was a fine adventure," he said of the experience.

Then, on February 8, 1951, Dr. W.E.B. DuBois

and other officers of the Peace Information Center were indicted by the Justice Department for failing to register the organization as an "agent for a foreign government." It was the beginning of the Communist witch-hunts in the United States.

Joseph McCarthy, a United States senator from Wisconsin, charged that he had secured a list of 205 government employees who were members of the Communist party. He claimed that the nation was at risk of being taken over by a foreign power. The "Red Scare" panicked otherwise clear-thinking people into irrational acts. People were turned in to the authorities for all kinds of suspicions, most of which were unfounded. Some people lost their jobs, their homes, and their families because of wild insinuations and innuendos. The "McCarthy Era" was an unprecedented period of national paranoia. Neighbors were suspicious of neighbors; friendships ended abruptly. Nobody wanted to be associated with anybody even remotely connected with the "C" word—Communism.

During the nine-month trial, Dr. DuBois answered that the Peace Information Center was not an organization designed to overthrow the United States government. The intent, he insisted, was "to tell the people of the United States what other nations were doing and thinking about war."

The case was dismissed when the judge ruled that the government had failed to prove its case that the Peace Information Center was an agent for a foreign government. The presiding judge, Matthew F. McGuire wrote: "The government has alleged that the Peace Information Center was the agent of a foreign principal. They proved the existence of the Peace Information Center. They certainly proved

the existence of the World Council of Peace . . .
But applying the test, as laid down here, in a case
which, presumably is the law of the land . . . in this
case, the government has failed to support on the
evidence adduced, the allegations laid down in the
indictment . . . So, therefore, the motion, under the
circumstances for a judgment of acquittal will be
granted."

DuBois made no secret about the fact that he
admired the Soviet government for its commitment
to racial harmony and equality, and he sincerely believed the Socialist party was an alternative to the
Democratic and Republican parties which had repeatedly failed African-Americans. But it could not
be proven that he was a traitor, and certainly not
the "agent" of any government. So what purpose
had the trial served?

DuBois was a world-renowned figure, highly respected and revered. The foreign press was appalled
when they learned how he had been treated like a
common criminal by his own government—hand-
cuffed, fingerprinted, and his apartment searched
for concealed weapons. The United States government also used blacklisting, censorship, and ha-
rassment to silence his supporters; such actions were
typical during the McCarthy witch-hunts.

Although DuBois was a strong person—physi-
cally and mentally—the ordeal took its toll. Dr.
DuBois was tired and no doubt it would have been
much harder for him if he hadn't had Shirley Graham DuBois, his new wife, to help him.

Shirley Graham had met DuBois when she was
a young girl, growing up in the Midwest. He had
visited her home during one of his lecture tours. She
had fallen in love with him then, and thirty years

later, she still loved him. Shirley Graham and W.E.B. DuBois were married two days prior to his indictment in 1951.

"We were free," she wrote after the acquittal. "That next afternoon we went home to 31 Grace Court [Brooklyn]." But, for the DuBoises, problems were far from over. In February 14, 1952, the United States State Department withheld their passports. The reason given was, "it appears that your proposed travel [to Rio de Janeiro] would be contrary to the best interest of the United States."[64]

Cut off from the world, unable to travel, DuBois threw all his energy into writing. He wrote letters, books, and commentaries. His first foray into fiction, the *Black Flame* trilogy, was written during this time. Critics vary in their appraisal of DuBois's fictional work, ranging from "complete failure," to "brilliant." Most literary scholars and students of DuBois quickly acknowledge that the three novels are not comparable to his scholarly works, but there is something very unique about the stories.

After years of scholarly writing, it was a new kind of writing for him, and he enjoyed the challenge of it. One biographer stated that the stories revealed "the violent antagonisms within DuBois that he had attempted to suppress during the years he sought racial equality by rational and scholarly means." *The Flame* trilogy allowed Dr. DuBois, through his characters' voices, to express feelings and emotions sub-

*Shirley Graham DuBois,*
*DuBois's second wife,*
*whom he married in 1951.*

jectively. In scholarly writing he had always tried to maintain objectivity. Writing fiction was a great release, especially following the terrible trial he had endured. And, it was a refreshing change for DuBois and his readers.[65]

While writing, Dr. DuBois also continued to work, on a nonsalaried basis, at the New York office of the Council on African Affairs, with Paul Robeson and W. Alphaeus Hunton.

"The Old Man" as he was affectionately called turned ninety in 1958. Many things were happening in the nation. The United States Supreme Court had reversed the *Plessy* v. *Ferguson* decision in the *Brown* v. *Board of Education of Topeka* decision of 1954. Joseph McCarthy had been censured by a 67 to 22 full Senate vote for his blatant misuse of power and authority. There had been a successful bus boycott in Montgomery, Alabama led by a young Baptist preacher named Rev. Dr. Martin Luther King, Jr. People were looking to Dr. King's new style of leadership—direct, nonviolent confrontation. Dr. DuBois was impressed with Martin Luther King and they had corresponded during the boycott.

It was in June of 1958 that the Supreme Court decided that a political affidavit was not necessary as a prerequisite for obtaining a passport. The DuBoises and Paul Robeson, whose travel also had been restricted, were free to travel again. The DuBoises left immediately for Europe on the luxury ship *Liberté*. His daughter, Yolande, came to see them off.

Dr. DuBois had been on trial in his own country, but he was a beloved world figure. The outpouring of respect and love for DuBois was moving and gratifying. He lectured and toured in European countries where he was greeted as both a scholar and humanitarian. His speeches were as fiery as ever; peace was his message, but he would not back down from his attacks on racism and discrimination wherever it was found—even in his own country.

On October 23, 1958, he was honored in Prague. Mrs. DuBois described the occasion:

> Before I was escorted to my place in the domed chambers, diplomats, foreign visitors, and friends filled the auditorium. Then from high overhead came a fanfare of trumpets, followed by music rolling from a great pipe organ. The audience rose to its feet and from the back, down the wide central aisle, marched a procession of medieval splendor, led by youths in scarlet and gold livery. Gorgeously clad professors and dons, men and women followed. And in the midst of all this pomp and circumstance, himself clothed in billowing robes and wearing an extremely chic black velvet hat, came the small, erect figure of W.E.B. DuBois, to receive the degree of Doctor of the Science of History, *honoris causa.*[66]

The University of Prague is one of the oldest universities in the world, and Dr. DuBois deeply appreciated the honorary degree. But it was in Berlin that DuBois, in another personally moving ceremony, received his Ph.D. from Berlin University (which had been renamed Humboldt University).

It was explained that Dr. DuBois's records had been preserved in the files. "We have taken them out," explained the Rector, "and carefully studied them. These records reveal the depth of this student's promise." And close to seventy years after his study in Berlin, DuBois was honored with the degree of Doctor of Economics. He responded, "Today you have fulfilled one of the highest ambitions of my young manhood."

From Berlin the DuBoises went to the Soviet Union, where they met with Soviet Premier Khrushchev briefly, then proceeded to China.

Mrs. DuBois wrote about the trip: "Our visit to China took place in the first quarter of 1959, when China was a highly controversial subject. Our visit was from the first of February to the last of April . . . During our visit my husband celebrated his ninety-first birthday." And the Chinese celebrated his birthday in grand style with feasting, dancing, singing, plays, and concerts.

In April, the couple returned to Moscow, where DuBois was given the Lenin Peace Prize, the highest honor awarded by the Soviet Union. It has rarely been given to a person who is not Russian.

A week after receiving the Lenin Peace Prize Dr. DuBois was in Stockholm attending the tenth anniversary of the World Peace Council. Then the DuBoises were on a plane back to London, where they were the guests of Paul Robeson and his wife.

Was this the schedule of a ninety-one-year-old man? Apparently DuBois was not a typical old man. His age did not dictate or limit his activities. He swam, walked, and kept pace with men and women half his age.

All too soon, it was time to come home. Mrs. DuBois wrote to the black American newspapers in the states, "We'll be home to celebrate the Fourth of July in our own backyard. Independence Day, Brother, and I mean INDEPENDENCE!"[67]

W.E.B. and Shirley returned to the United States only to learn that their passports were again being taken by the State Department. So the next year was spent quietly at home in Brooklyn, New York. He wrote, lectured when he was invited, read, and watched television. "Perry Mason" was one of his favorite programs.

The world had changed so much since his birth in 1868, yet changes in race relations were sometimes barely noticeable. DuBois was well aware of the nonviolent movement materializing in the South. He watched with interest Martin Luther King, Jr., and praised the young civil rights leader for being "honest, straightforward, well trained, and knowing the limits." But for the most part, DuBois did not participate in any movements. He wasn't tired or angry as some speculated; he hadn't turned his back on the race. W.E.B. DuBois was busy doing what he had set out to do as a young man—research and writing. And for the moment he was content.

# thirteen

## THE FINAL YEARS

In 1960 the DuBoises' passports were returned and immediately they traveled to Ghana. He welcomed the opportunity to work on an *Encyclopedia Africana* commissioned by President Kwame Nkrumah. Ghana was free from European rule, and because of his long work in the Pan-African Movement, W.E.B. DuBois was a national hero. President Nkrumah was trying desperately to establish a proud, strong, and independent nation equal to the historical Ghana of long ago. Who better could help him than DuBois? Nkrumah invited his lifelong friend to come and live in Ghana.

Leaving the United States didn't take much consideration. DuBois returned to the United States to take care of unfinished business. He had made the decision, but he had to act on that decision much sooner than he'd anticipated. Through the grapevine, it was rumored that the State Department was going to seize their passports again. The DuBoises made a hasty departure, but not before Dr. DuBois took one more defiant action, and officially joined the Communist Party.

In a letter to Gus Hall, chairman of the Communist Party in the United States, Dr. DuBois ap-

*DuBois in 1961, two years
before his death. DuBois devoted
his final years to compiling the
Encyclopedia Africana. To the
end he was first and foremost
a scholar and a teacher.*

plied for membership saying, "I have been long and slow in coming to this conclusion, but at last my mind is settled." Then he listed ten demands he felt would "provide the United States with a real Third party, and thus restore democracy to this land."

1. Public ownership of natural resources and of all capital.
2. Public ownership of transportation and communications.
3. Abolition of poverty and limitation of personal income.
4. No exploitation of labor.
5. Social medicine, with hospitalization and care of the old.
6. Free education for all.
7. Training for jobs and jobs for all.
8. Discipline for growth and reform.
9. Freedom under law.
10. No dogmatic religion.

"These aims are not crimes," he said in the conclusion of his letter. "They are practiced increasingly all over the world. No nation can call itself free which does not allow its citizens to work for these ends."[68]

Two hundred people showed up at the airport to say good-bye to him. He smiled, waved, and at ninety-three turned toward a new life. After a year, he became a citizen of Ghana.

The question of why DuBois left America to live his final days basking in the adoration heaped on him by his new countrymen is moot. He was heralded the "father of African nationalism." And until his death in 1963 his days were filled with work and peace. He was surrounded by love, free to work, think, feel, and live life on his own terms, unlimited by race hatred and discrimination.

When he died at age ninety-five, Ghana gave him a state funeral. Details of his funeral made headlines in major international capitals. Ghanan schools and public offices were closed. Schoolchildren sang praise songs, and women and children wept openly for him. His body was laid to rest fifty yards from the "pounding surf, beside the wall of the Castle," residence of the president of Ghana.

A letter he had written, dated June 26, 1957, was read after his death to all those who had come to mourn. The following is an excerpt:

"I have loved my work, I have loved people and my play, but always I have been uplifted by the thought that what I have done well will live long and justify my life; that what I have done and will never finish can now be handed on to others for endless days to be finished, perhaps better than I could have done."[69]

# EPILOGUE:
# THE BLACK FLAME
# STILL BURNS

In America there were no headlines, no school-children sang, there was no massive outpouring of love for W.E.B. DuBois. In fact, most schoolchildren didn't know who he was. When the death announcement was made at the 1963 March on Washington there were many who turned to one another asking, "Who was he?" The irony, of course, is that it was he who had paved the road that had led most of the demonstrators to Washington on that day.

Unfortunately, too many Americans believe the civil rights movement began in the 1960s and that Martin Luther King, Jr., was the first and principal leader. The work of King and the contemporary civil rights leaders cannot be diminished, but their efforts should be viewed from a proper historical perspective. They were building on the work of others.

The battle for freedom began in 1619, when the first African-Americans were herded on boats, transported, and sold into bondage. Without understanding the struggles of men and women like Nat Turner, Harriet Tubman, Sojourner Truth, Frederick Douglass, T. Thomas Fortune, William Monroe Trotter, Mary Church Terrell, Carter Woodson,

Langston Hughes, Marcus Garvey, and others, the civil rights movement of the 1960s would seem empty and disconnected.

W.E.B. DuBois's place in American history is critical. During his lifetime man went from traveling on horseback to soaring in jets, from cooking in a fireplace to fast-food restaurants. He was the living link between two key civil rights leaders—Frederick Douglass and Martin Luther King, Jr., both of whom he knew.

Writer Virginia Hamilton calls Dr. DuBois the single most important civil rights leader of the twentieth century. Broderick summarized his biography of DuBois with, "The austere Dr. DuBois reminded Negro intellectuals that courage and talent could carry a man—and a race—far." And to this Moore adds, "he carved his initials in the universe."

Another way to summarize his work is with a Chinese parable: Once there was a man who lived in the shadow of a great mountain. The mountain blocked the sunlight and stopped the rains from falling on his crops. One day the man decided to move the mountain. With a shovel and bucket he began to scoop the earth and rocks and move it bucket by bucket, day by day.

One morning a wise man came by and said to the man, "Fool! Don't you know you can't move the mountain with a shovel and bucket. It is nonsense!"

But the man replied, "I may not be able to move the mountain, but if my sons and daughters see me trying they will be inspired. They, too, will move the mountain bucket by bucket, day by day, and so will their sons and daughters . . . and their sons and daughters. And so the mountain will be moved."

Crowds jam the area around the Lincoln
Memorial during the March on Washington on
August 28, 1963, the day after DuBois died in
Ghana, West Africa. At the time, few could
appreciate all that he had done to bring America
to this moment.

That is the legacy of Dr. W.E.B. DuBois. He encouraged his people to move the mountain of injustice, race hatred, and discrimination, never yielding to anything less than completion. The Black Flame still burns.

# APPENDIX:
# THE WRITINGS OF
# W.E.B. DUBOIS

The Suppression of the African Slave Trade to the United States of America, 1638–1870 (1896)

Atlanta University Studies on the American Negro (1897–1915)

The Philadelphia Negro (1899)

The Souls of Black Folk (1903).

John Brown—a biography (1909)

The Quest of the Silver Fleece—a novel (1911)

The Negro (1915)

Darkwater: Voices from Within the Veil (1920)

The Gift of Black Folk: The Negroes in the Making of America, (1924)

Dark Princess—A romance novel (1928)

Black Reconstruction in America, 1869–1880 (1935)

Black Folk: Then and Now (1939)

Dusk of Dawn: An Essay Toward an Autobiography of a Race Concept—an autobiographical essay (1940)

*Color and Democracy: Colonies and Peace* (1945)

*The World and Africa* (1946)

*In Battle for Peace: The Story of My 83rd Birthday—*
An autobiographical essay (1952)

*The Black Flame: a Trilogy*
*The Ordeal of Mansart* (1957)
*Mansart Builds a School* (1959)
*Worlds of Color* (1964)
*The Autobiography of* W.E.B. *DuBois* (1963)
*An ABC of Color* (1964)

# SOURCE NOTES

## CHAPTER ONE

1. Francis L. Broderick. *W.E.B. DuBois—Negro Leader in a Time of Crisis*, p. 1.
2. DuBois, Shirley, *DuBois: A Pictorial Biography*, p. 2.
3. Ibid., p. 3.
4. Ibid., p. 4.
5. Ibid., p. 4.
6. Broderick, p. 4–5.
7. Ibid., p. 3.
8. Ibid., p. 7.

## CHAPTER TWO

9. Lerone Bennett. *Before the Mayflower—a History of Black America*, p. 145.
10. Broderick, p. 9.
11. Ibid., p. 10.
12. Ibid., p. 7.
13. Ibid., p. 10.
14. W.E.B. DuBois. *The Souls of Black Folk*, p. xxiii.
15. Broderick, p. 11.
16. Ibid., p. 9.
17. Ibid., p. 10.
18. DuBois, Shirley, p. 8.

## CHAPTER THREE

19. Ibid., p. 12.
20. World Book, Vol. H, "Harvard."

21. DuBois, Shirley, p. 10.
22. Ibid., p. 10.
23. Biographical Dictionary. "William James."
24. DuBois, Shirley, p. 12.
25. DuBois, W.E.B., *The Autobiography of W.E.B. DuBois*, p. 25.
26. Ibid., p. 36.
27. Broderick, p. 19–20.
28. Moore, Jack. *W.E.B. DuBois*, p. 32.
29. DuBois, Shirley, p. 13.
30. Broderick, p. 21.
31. Moore, p. 39.

**CHAPTER FOUR**

32. Adams, Russell. *Great Negroes Past and Present*, p. 115.
33. DuBois, Shirley, p. 22.
34. Moore, p. 44.
35. Broderick, p. 32.
36. DuBois, Shirley, p. 24.
37. DuBois, W.E.B., p. 226-232.
38. McKissack, Patricia and Fredrick. *The Civil Rights Movement in America from 1865–Present*, p. 135.
39. Bennett, p. 319.

**CHAPTER FIVE**

40. DuBois, Shirley, p. 35–40.
41. McKissack, Patricia and Fredrick, pp. 133–147.
42. Ibid., p. 147.
43. World Book, Vol. W, "Booker T. Washington."
44. Bennett, p. 317.

**CHAPTER SIX**

45. DuBois, W.E.B., *Souls of Black Folk*, p. xxiii.

**CHAPTER SEVEN**

46. Broderick, p. 76–78.
47. Bennett, p. 337.
48. Broderick, p. 77.
49. Bennett, p. 338–338.
50. Ibid., p. 339.
51. Moore, p. 60

## CHAPTER EIGHT

52. Broderick, p. 128.
53. DuBois, Shirley, p. 52.
54. Adams, Russell, p. 115.
55. Ibid., p. 115.

## CHAPTER NINE

56. DuBois, Shirley, p. 57.
57. Ibid., pp. 60–64.

## CHAPTER TEN

58. DuBois, W.E.B., *Autobiography of W.E.B. DuBois*, p. 52.
59. Adams, Russell, "Walter White," p. 218.

## CHAPTER ELEVEN

60. Aptheker, Herbert., *The Correspondence of W.E.B. DuBois.*, Vol. III, p. 152.
61. Ibid., p. 152.
62. Adams, Russell, "Paul Robeson," p. 115.
63. Ibid., p. 115.

## CHAPTER TWELVE

64. DuBois, Shirley, pp. 82–88.
65. Moore, p. 71.
66. DuBois, Shirley, p. 118.
67. p. 135.

## CHAPTER THIRTEEN

68. Aptheker, Herbert., Vol. III, p. 8.
69. DuBois, Shirley, p. 167.

# BIBLIOGRAPHY

Adams, Russell. *Great Negroes Past and Present*. New York: Afro-Am Publishing Company, 1985.

Aptheker, Herbert. ed. *The Correspondence of W.E.B. DuBois*. Vols. I, II, and III. Boston: University of Massachusetts Press, 1976.

Bennett, Lerone. *Before the Mayflower—A History of Black America*. Chicago: Johnson Publishing Company, 1987.

Broderick, Francis L. *W.E.B. DuBois—Negro Leader in a Time of Crisis*. Stanford, California: Stanford University Press, 1959.

DuBois, Shirley Graham. *DuBois: A Pictorial Biography*. Chicago, Illinois: Johnson Publishing Company, 1978.

DuBois, Shirley Graham. *His Day is Marching On: A Memoir of W.E.B. DuBois*. Philadelphia: Lippincott, 1971.

DuBois, W.E.B. *Against Racism*. Amherst: University of Massachusetts Press, 1985.

DuBois, W.E.B. *In Battle for Peace*. Millwood, New York: Kraus-Thomson Organization Limited, 1976.

DuBois, W.E.B. *The Souls of Black Folk*. New York: New American Library Press, Reprint 1969.

Hughes, Langston, Milton Meltzer and E. Eric Lincoln. *A Pictorial History of Black Americans*. New York: Crown Publishing Company, 1983.

McKissack, Patricia and Fredrick. *The Civil Rights Movement in America from 1865 to Present.* Chicago: Children's Press, 1985.

Moore, Jack B. *W.E.B. DuBois.* Boston: Twayne Publishers, 1981.

Rampersad, Arnold. *The Art and Imagination of W.E.B. DuBois.* Cambridge: Harvard University Press, 1976.

Tuttle, William M., ed. *W.E.B. DuBois.* Great Lives Observed Series. Englewood Cliffs, New Jersey: Prentice-Hall, 1973.

# INDEX

Harlan, Louis, 56, 58, 64
Harlem, 91
*Harlem Shadows* (McKay),
  91–92
Harpers Ferry, West Virginia,
  68
Harvard, John, 29
Harvard University, 28–37
Hayes, Rutherford B., 36, 47
Hershaw, L. M., 69
Hope, John, 100
*Horizon, The*, 69, 71, 73, 75
Hosmer, Frank S., 17
Hughes, Langston, 92–93,
  130
Hunton, Alphaeus, 113, 120

Imperialism, 37, 79

James, William, 30, 32
Johnson, Jack, 71
Johnson, James Weldon, 87–
  88, 91, 98

King, Martin Luther, Jr., 120,
  123, 129, 130
Ku Klux Klan, 69, 80, 114

Lampman, Sally, 12
Lenin Peace Prize, 122
Liberia, 84
Lincoln, Abraham, 26
Lincoln College, 22
Lynching, 107–108, 110

McCarthy, Joseph, 116, 120
McGuire, Matthew F., 116–
  117
McKay, Claude, 92
Miller, Kelly, 59
Monroe, James, 84
Moore, Jack B., 43, 64
Morris, William, 22
Motherwit, 33

National Association for the
  Advancement of Colored
  People (NAACP), 83, 86
  DuBois's involvement
    with, 73–75, 87–89, 98–
    101, 103, 105, 107–108,
    112
  founding of, 74–75
  membership decline in, 95
  on Pan-African
    Movement, 87–88
  on segregation, 98–99
National Emergency
  Committee Against Mob
  Violence, 107
Native Americans, 47
*Negro, The* (DuBois), 78
Niagara Movement, 67–71, 73
Nkrumah, Kwame, 125

"Open Letter to the Southern
  People, An" (DuBois), 26
Ovington, Mary, 73, 100

Pan-African Congress of 1900,
  79
Pan-African Congress of 1921,
  83
Pan-African Congress of 1945,
  105
Pan-African Movement, 78–
  79, 87–88
Peace Information Center,
  115–116
"Philadelphia Negro, A Social
  Study, The" (DuBois), 43
"Plantation and Peasant
  Proprietorship Systems of
  Agriculture in the Southern
  United States, The"
  (DuBois), 39
Plessy, Homer, 48
*Plessy v. Ferguson*, 48, 120
*Pylon, The*, 100–101

# ABOUT THE AUTHORS

Patricia and Fredrick McKissack are a wife-and-husband writing team. They are recipients of the prestigious Coretta Scott King Award from the American Library Association. Pat holds a B.A. in English from Tennessee State University and a master's degree in children's literature from Webster University. Her book *Flossie and the Fox* was selected as a best book of 1986 by *School Library Journal* and a Best Children's Book selection by *Time*. Fred holds a B.S. in civil engineering from Tennessee State University. He has a strong interest in sports of all kinds. Pat and Fred McKissack have three sons. They make their home in the St. Louis area. Their joint hobby is gardening.